FURNITURE MAKING

A Manual of Techniques

ANTHONY HONTOIR

The Crowood Press

First published in 1989 by
The Crowood Press
Ramsbury, Marlborough
Wiltshire SN8 2HE

British Library Cataloguing in Publication Data

Hontoir, Anthony
    Furniture making.
    1. Furniture. Making – Amateurs' manuals
    I. Title
    684.1

    ISBN 1 85223 195 5

All photographs and line-drawings by the author.

Typeset by Acorn Bookwork, Salisbury, Wilts
Printed and bound in Great Britain by
Courier International Ltd, Tiptree, Essex

Contents

Introduction

The skill of the cabinet-maker has been handed down through the generations for hundreds of years, and will endure as long as there is a demand for high-quality handmade furniture. In fact, this skill is probably of greater significance now than it has ever been in the past, because so much of the mass-produced furniture in this present age is singularly lacking in grace and refinement. The craftsmen who left us such a rich heritage of classic styles in chairs, tables and cabinets have long since gone, but fortunately there is a strong revival of interest in the methods they employed and the results that were obtained.

In this book I aim to show you how the various techniques passed on over the generations can be learned and applied to the most practical and enjoyable pastime of making your own furniture. It is inevitable that we should turn to the past in our search for inspired elegance and, not surprisingly, many of the pieces that emerge from the work-bench after hours of intricate work are founded in a different period of history, and are generally known as reproduction furniture.

Such a title bears heavy responsibility, for in any type of reproduction work the cabinet-maker usually faces a dilemma. Should the piece merely look authentic, or ought it to be correct in every aspect of its general design and proportions? The answer is often a compromise, balancing what amounts to a personal opinion of refined good taste with something that is practical and possible.

For instance, there is a strong argument in favour of merging various periods to produce a piece which has a mixture of styles. Does this matter? The purist might object, but if the result is an item of furniture that is at once pleasing to behold and serves a useful purpose into the bargain, then the merging of periods has surely been proved a success. After all, history is a series of events, each one adding to that which went immediately before. Every period has borrowed from those that preceded it, so why should we suddenly raise objections now? In attempting to reproduce a flavour of the past, is it not right to savour only the best, while the remainder is allowed to disappear quietly into the shadows of time?

The examples depicted in this book are mostly of a reproduction style, but there is no attempt to pass them off as antiques. Instead, they are designs which are capable of giving much pleasure and satisfaction when you live with them from day to day.

It is the ambition of most woodworkers as they progress in their knowledge of the craft to explore the various woods that have an established reputation. But times change, and certain species that were once commonly available are not now so plentiful, whilst other types have taken their place. We stand today facing the dawn of a new ecological enlightenment, knowing that the world's tropical rain forests are being depleted at such a rate that their rapid loss is affecting the balance of nature with dire consequences.

Fortunately, this need not deter the cabinet-maker. A wealth of fine wood can be salvaged from old unwanted furniture if you take the time and trouble to search through the attic, scour the second-hand market and attend local auctions. Over the years I have picked up countless items for ridiculously low prices and turned them into new tables and cabinets. All the oak and mahogany that I use has been rescued and it is nearly always of excellent quality.

This book has deliberately kept off the subject of veneering, partly because it is a technique which demands special attention and skill, and partly due to the fact that there is an unspoken preference among furniture-makers for using only solid wood, with the exception of employing a limited amount of plywood.

The measurements quoted throughout the book are given both in imperial and metric. Many people still prefer to work in inches, especially when it is a matter of a lifetime's familiarity; and there is something perverse about using millimetres to practise a traditional craft. Therefore, I have placed the imperial system first, followed by metric. If you attempt to convert from one system of measurement to the other midway through a piece, you will encounter unavoidable discrepancies, and may wonder if there is some underlying fault in the method of conversion. There is not. If you check on a tape-measure which is graduated in inches and in millimetres, you will find that the millimetres are taken to the nearest convenient number.

Little more need be said by way of introduction. The following pages will lead you through the most important stages in learning how to make furniture. Beyond that, all future success must remain in your own hands.

1 Making a Workshop

Most of us are able to find somewhere suitable around the house to set up a small workshop without causing great inconvenience. For the majority, it will be at the far end of the garage, or inside the garden shed, while for the fortunate few who reside in large properties, there is always a spare room somewhere which can be converted into a workplace.

Once you have established your own little niche, you will need to make provision for a good, effective working surface, usually in the form of a sturdy bench, for a means of storing all your woodworking tools, and to have sufficient space available for keeping a stock of timber ready for use. You will also need enough room to work comfortably without falling over things every time you move.

As a last resort there is always the kitchen table, upon which some of the finest pieces of work are reputed to have originated! The kitchen table does, of course, have severe limitations, but if you are prepared to clamp a piece of worktop material on to the table and fit a small detachable vice to the front edge, you do, indeed, have the basis of a temporary workshop.

It is inside the garage or the garden shed, however, that most amateur woodworkers set up their woodworking facilities. My own work-bench has occupied part of the garage for a number of years, with the advantage of a good solid floor laid in concrete, plenty of light and a power supply. No piece of work has ever been too big to tackle, because once the car has been removed and the entire floor area cleared, there is more than enough space available.

If you choose to work in a small wooden shed, check that the floor has sufficient strength to withstand the weight of the work-bench, and if necessary reinforce it with additional timbers. You may be able to run a power supply from the house, but electrical work of this sort is best left to a competent electrician. The same applies to the installing of an electric light.

THE WORK-BENCH

Construction

It is important to choose the right type of work-bench, because this has a direct bearing on the quality of the work you produce. Although there are plenty of good portable work-benches on the market, the serious woodworker generally needs something that is larger, has a proper carpenter's vice attached to it, and a top surface that is wide and deep enough to allow for the making of sizeable items with plenty of space to work easily.

The work-bench shown overleaf follows the traditional pattern of having four stout legs joined together by rails; the top front rail is particularly deep to provide a

Cutting List

Leg: four of 30 × 2¾ × 2¾in (762 × 70 × 70mm)

Top skirt rail: one of 48 × 6 × 1½in (1,220 × 152 × 38mm)

Top back rail: one of 48 × 3 × 1½in (1,220 × 76 × 38mm)

Top side rail: two of 22¼ × 3 × 1½in (565 × 76 × 38mm)

Bottom front and back rail: two of 42¼ × 3 × 1½in (1,072 × 76 × 38mm)

Bottom side rail: two of 21½ × 3 × 1½in (547 × 76 × 38mm)

Main work-bench top: one of 48 × 15 × ⅞in (1,220 × 380 × 22mm)

Rear work-bench top: one of 48 × 4 × ⅞in (1,220 × 102 × 22mm)

Plywood tool tray: one of 48 × 6 × ½in (1,220 × 152 × 13mm)

Bottom plywood panel: one of 42¼ × 23 × ½in (1,072 × 584 × 13mm)

Wedge: two of 4⅛ × 3 × ⅞in (105 × 76 × 22mm)

The traditional carpenter's work-bench is essential for providing a good solid working surface large enough to cope with most types of furniture-making.

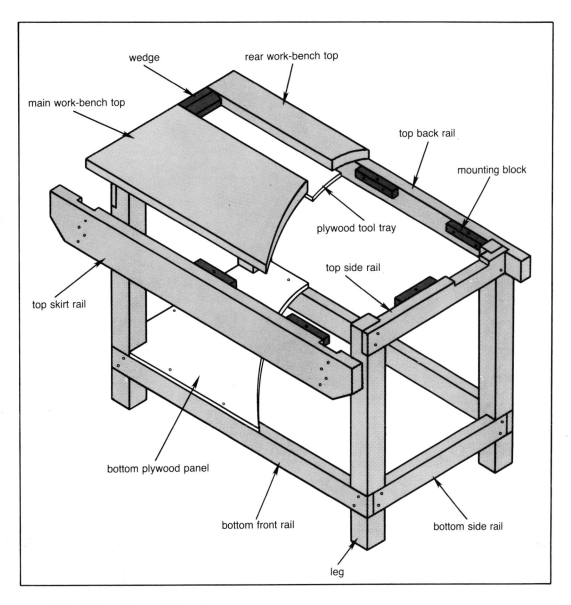

An exploded view of the work-bench.

skirt in which the vice is mounted. The working surface is a thick piece of hardwood which has a recessed tool tray fitted towards the rear. The bottom rails support the lower shelf, which is cut from plywood and used to store materials and certain large tools.

The construction of the work-bench is quite straightforward, since it makes use of the halved joint throughout. The frame is made from softwood, and the hardwood top may be any good-quality wood such as beech or oak. The lower shelf and tool tray are both cut from ½in (13mm)-thick birch-faced plywood.

Take four lengths of 2¾ × 2¾in (70 × 70mm) timber and square off the ends to give a length of 30in (762mm) each. Cut

11

these to size and mark them for the halved joints with the rails (*see* below). Strictly speaking, the joints are not true halves, since the legs are substantially thicker than the rails.

All the rails are half-jointed in position, with the single exception of the top front skirt rail. The four bottom rails are mounted 4in (100mm) up from the ground to support the bottom shelf, and the three remaining rails are located at the top, consisting of two sides and one back rail.

In common with the skirt rail, the corresponding top back rail overhangs the workbench by 3in (75mm) at either end, but the rest of the rails fit flush into the outer corner of each leg.

All the rails have a common thickness of 1¾in (38mm), and it is this that governs the depth of the joints, which are simply arranged as follows: a ¾in (19mm)-thick portion is cut from the end of a rail, and a corresponding ¾in (19mm)-deep recess cut in the leg so that the two parts fit perfectly together, the side of the rail lying flush with the side or edge of the leg.

Start by cutting the recesses for the bottom shelf rails in all four legs. Mark in their positions with the square, setting a distance of 3in (75mm) between the lines equal to the width of the rails. Set the marking gauge to ¾in (19mm) and inscribe the depth lines for each joint.

Cut the joints by firstly sawing down the sides of the squared lines as far as the gauged depth line using the tenon saw, then chisel away all the waste. When you have completed one joint section on the side of the leg, mark out an identical halved section on the adjacent edge for the second rail, using the same tools and method to cut it.

Next, prepare the halved joints in the rails. Note that the front and back rails run the full 2¾in (70mm) width of the leg, whereas the side rails are cut short to 2in (50mm). This avoids the unnecessary and time-consuming practice of cutting mitres at the ends of all the rails.

When the bottom shelf joints are complete, repeat a similar procedure for the top back and top side rails. In this case, though, the rails each lie flush with the top of the legs and the back rail overhangs at each end, so it is notched with two ¾in (19mm)-deep recesses to fit the joints. The front surfaces of the two front legs are left untouched for the fitting of the skirt rail, but the rail itself is notched with two ½in (13mm)-deep recesses to allow it to fit in position and give added strength to the structure.

Test all the joints for accuracy by loosely assembling the work-bench frame, and prepare them for final assembly by drilling two countersunk number 8 screw holes per joint to take 2in (50mm) woodscrews. The wide front skirt rail is the only exception, being fixed with four stronger 3in (75mm) number 10 woodscrews per joint.

Mix a quantity of wood glue in a suitable vessel (such as an old cup), and assemble the sides first, gluing and screwing the joints together. When these are complete, but before fitting the front and back rails in position, measure for the tool tray. This consists of a 48in (1,220mm) length of ½in (13mm)-thick plywood fully recessed into the two top edges of the upper side rails, 6in (150mm) in width, set at a distance of 4in (100mm) from the rear. Mark in these recesses and remove the waste wood using the tenon saw, chisel and mallet.

Now complete the framework assem-

Assembling the frame of the work-bench consists of joining the rails to the legs, starting with the two end frame assemblies before attaching the front and back rails, finishing with the top front skirt rail.

bly by fitting the front and back rails; *but do not glue the skirt rail* – screw it in place only. The reason for this is that the longer and bigger screws hold it more effectively, and if it becomes necessary or desirable at any future time to replace the vice, the rail can easily be removed.

The Working Surface

Having finished the major assembly, the work-bench now has to be fitted with its working surface, and the vice installed on the front skirt. This brings us to the subject of acquiring a suitable piece of hardwood for the top.

The top should ideally be cut from a piece of beech, but it would be terribly expensive to purchase enough of it from the timber merchant to make a good, strong bench top. A far better idea is to get hold of some old furniture and salvage a board that is sufficiently long and wide to serve as the top.

The working surface for example shown on page 10 was originally a solid oak headboard, measuring 7⁄8in (22mm) thick, and it only needed to be cut to 48in (1,220m) in length and 15³⁄8in (390mm) in width to form the main surface. The narrower strip at the rear is 4½in (115mm) wide. The two pieces are best machined to remove a thin layer from the top surface, thus exposing a clean fresh layer of oak beneath, which is natural in colour.

The work-bench top is fixed to the frame using small beech mounting blocks, seven in number, spaced around the inside of the frame. The eighth mounting block is much larger, and serves to mount the vice as well.

Cut the seven blocks, each 6in (150mm) in length, from scrap material measuring approximately 1¼ × ¾in (32 × 19mm). It does not have to be beech – any good hardwood will do. Drill each block with two number 8 holes through the edge to screw it to the frame, and a single hole passing upwards through the side to screw into the underside of the worktop. Countersink all three holes, then glue and screw each block in place.

The Vice

The vice comes next. Deciding exactly which is the best type of woodworking vice for your own requirements is not easy. There are a number of models on the market, varying greatly in price according to size, quality and strength. An expensive, strong model will undeniably give you many years of reliable service; but you could pay a lot less and settle for a cheaper vice which is more than adequate for amateur use. Your final decision depends on how much you are likely to use the vice, and whether or not you plan to carry out mainly heavy carpentry and joinery, or light woodwork and cabinet-making. I would advise you to opt for the most expensive model you can afford – it will probably pay off in the long run.

As there are many different sizes and types of vice available, it is beyond the scope of this book to give precise fitting instructions, but you can rest assured that the average woodworking vice requires only reasonable common sense to be fitted securely in position. Broadly speaking, this is what it involves. The body of the vice is placed against the inside of the front skirt, usually on the

left-hand side of the work-bench, and its position marked. Three or four large diameter holes are drilled for the screw-thread and sliding bars, the fourth optional hole depending on the presence of a quick-release mechanism. The body is screwed securely to the bench.

A large wooden spacer block is cut substantially bigger than the body of the vice and fitted to it with four nuts, bolts and washers, sinking the nuts into recessed holes. The block is then drilled with six screw holes and screwed tightly up against the underside of the worktop. Place the work-bench top in position and mark the various screw holes. Drill a pilot hole for each one, and finally screw the top down.

Finishing the Work-Bench

Cut a length of plywood to fit the tool tray recess, slide it into place and screw it to the underside of the worktop. Then fit the rear top portion and secure likewise.

Complete the top surface by fitting two softwood wedges at either end of the tool tray to prevent small objects from accidentally rolling off. These wedges should be of the same thickness as the bench top, and can easily be sawn and planed to fit. They are screwed to the plywood from the underside.

Cut a large sheet of ½in (13mm) plywood to make the bottom shelf, removing square pieces from all four corners to fit around the legs. Fix in place with twelve 1½in (38mm) number 8 woodscrews.

All that remains is to fit wooden cheeks to the sliding jaw of the vice and the corresponding position on the skirt rail. Once again, beech is preferable, but oak will do. Trim two pieces to fit, and screw in place.

The woodworker's vice.

A final detail is a bench stop. You can buy these quite cheaply in the form of small metal flaps which are set flush into the top of the work-bench and raised or lowered as required. A simpler idea is to chisel out a square hole in the surface, rather as if you were cutting a stopped mortise, and knock a square hardwood block into the hole so that it protrudes 1in (25mm) above the work surface.

Either way, a bench stop is essential for planing operations and should be fitted. If you happen to be left-handed, it is better placed on the right side of the bench; otherwise it should go in the usual position somewhere behind the vice.

MAKING THE MOST OF THE WORK-BENCH

A good, solid carpenter's work-bench provides you with a firm foundation for all your woodworking activities, but it can be made far more versatile so that you can cope with virtually any requirement.

Most vice-work is confined to handling relatively small sections of wood, often simply cutting mortises and tenons, sawing halved joints, drilling holes and holding the workpiece upright for cutting dovetails. But occasionally you will find that the vice is called upon to hold a particularly long length of wood, per-

A dowel peg inserted into a hole drilled through the skirt rail and into the leg at the opposite end to the vice serves to support long pieces of wood and prevent them from dropping under their own weight.

15

haps a door stile or something of a similar size. The piece projects so far beyond the vice that its weight tends to make it drop down at its unsupported end. Consequently, it can prove very difficult to plane along its entire length. The wood obviously needs to be held up at its far end.

The best way of supporting it is to cut a 6in (150mm)-long wooden peg from a length of ⅝in (16mm)-diameter hardwood dowelling. Insert this into a hole drilled for the purpose in the skirt rail on the right side of the work-bench, where it should pass into the leg. In fact, two holes should be drilled in order to give two alternative heights, both being bored to a depth of 2in (50mm) through the skirt and into the right-hand front leg. The lower hole is arranged to coincide with the level of the vice's sliding bars, and the second hole is positioned higher up to give an optional support for narrower sections of wood.

The Bench Hook

There are instances when it is either too awkward to hold a piece of wood in the vice, or impossible, owing to its shape or size. This is where the bench hook comes in, proving itself indispensable as a work-bench accessory.

All you need to make your own bench hook is a flat base of hardwood measuring 8in (200mm) long and 5in (125mm) wide. A piece of ¾in (19mm)-thick oak is ideal for this purpose. A block of ash or beech is dowel-jointed and glued flush with each end, one on the top, the other on the bottom. Each block is 4in (100mm) long and measures ⅞ × ⅞in (22 × 22mm) in cross-section. Both pieces are fitted to the base of the bench hook in such a way

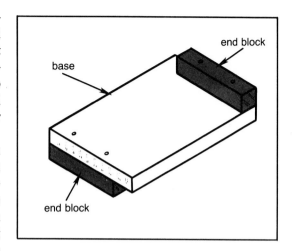

The bench hook.

that 1in (25mm) of the base projects at the side. One block is located fully to the left, the other fully to the right so that left-handed and right-handed users are both accommodated.

G-Clamps

If you need to hold a large, flat piece of wood steady, either to saw along its length or to work a special groove or edging along or across the grain with a plough plane or router, the wood must be clamped at the side of the work-bench so that it overhangs by the required amount. The most suitable method of clamping it in this position is to employ a pair of strong G-clamps, one placed at either end, with a length of scrap wood acting as a protective spacer between the wood and the foot of the clamp.

The Vertical Drill Stand

For a great many drilling jobs it is easy to get into the habit of using an electric drill to bore holes in a piece of wood held in the vice, holding the drill free-hand. This is all very well if you have a firm, steady grip and a straight eye, but what if the hole must be drilled at exact right-angles, to a pre-determined depth? Can you be sure that your hands and your eyes can achieve such a high degree of accuracy?

The answer for most of us is 'no', and usually it is a mistake to assume that you can match the precision of a machine without some assistance. The best tool accessory for this purpose is the vertical drill stand, which will prove invaluable if you have a large number of holes to drill with great precision. There are various drill stands available, and you should be able to find one that matches your particular drill. They all work on the same principle of clamping the drill upright in

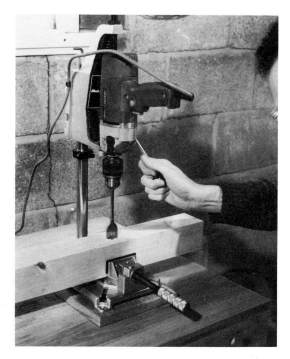

The vertical drill stand is bolted securely to the top of the work-bench, providing a precise means of drilling holes.

its holder, and lowering it on to the workpiece by pulling down on a lever. Some drill stands have a scale marked on them to indicate the distance travelled by the drill, and an adjustable stop to prevent you from drilling any further than you want.

The drill stand needs to be fixed very securely to the top of the work-bench, preferably by cutting out a wooden mounting panel to which the base of the stand is screwed. A small block of wood is glued to the underside of this panel, identical in size to the square hole cut in the top of the work-bench to receive the bench stop.

This enables the panel to be positioned on the work-bench above the place where the bench stop usually fits, and held there. The method of holding it is to drill a ⅜in (9mm)-diameter hole through the panel, the block and the bench stop recess, so that a bolt can be passed through to lock the panel to the bench surface, the end of the bolt being fastened with a washer and wing-nut beneath the bench top.

Screw the base of the drill stand to the wooden panel, mount the electric drill, and you are ready to begin drilling your holes with controlled precision. A small vice may be mounted on the drill stand to hold the workpiece steady.

The Lathe Accessory

If one of your aims is to practise the skilled craft of wood-turning but you cannot afford to buy a fully-equipped lathe, you could instead purchase a lathe accessory for your drill. It consists of a long channelled base which is screwed down to the top of the workbench, preferably at the back, and into this channel slots the headstock, tool rest and tail-stock assemblies. The electric drill fits into the headstock, where it provides the motive power for the lathe.

It would, of course, be wrong to anticipate the same scope from this simple drill attachment compared with either a miniature bench-mounted lathe or a much larger and more sophisticated cabinet-type lathe, but if you only expect to turn the occasional piece of wood, this accessory is a worthwhile investment and one that further extends the range of the drill's capabilities. It also helps you to become familiar with wood-turning techniques before paying a larger sum of money for a more elaborate lathe.

SAFETY PRECAUTIONS

Perhaps you can devise a few other uses for your work-bench, to suit your own special needs. Whatever you do, remember that the woodworker's bench is a place where you manipulate sharp tools and handle high-speed mechanical saws and drills. Always take adequate safety precautions – such as the wearing of protective goggles to cover your eyes, a face mask to avoid inhaling fine dust particles, and ear-muffs to safeguard your hearing from the loud whine of an electric planer, router or jigsaw. Dressed in all this, you will probably be hard to recognise! Above all, keep your hands well back from fast-moving machinery.

Switch off power tools and remove them from their stands when they are not in use, and always replace your tools neatly in their storage racks rather than leave them lying around to clutter the place up. Never let wood shavings or sawdust accumulate on the work-bench or the surrounding floor, because they are a potential fire risk as well as a menace for slipping on.

With a little imagination and proper care, the work-bench and the rest of your workshop facilities should provide you with many hours of pleasure, and hopefully some fine pieces of woodwork will emerge as a result.

THE TOOL CABINET

Construction

All woodworking tools must be carefully looked after if they are to produce good results, and this means keeping them clean and sharp, and storing them away correctly when not in use. The most practical method of storage is the tool cabinet, which can be hung on the wall near your place of work.

There is no set size or pattern of cabinet to which you must conform, but certain details of layout are generally accepted. The overall dimensions should bear some relation to the number of tools you intend storing in it. The design above shows a medium-sized cabinet with two doors, and an interior of shelves, racks, special retainers, hooks and a useful drawer. The internal features can, of course, be altered to provide more storage space for some tools and less for others, according to your own requirements. If you have yet to build up your tool outfit, you should wait until you have amassed a dozen items or more before planning your cabinet.

The main components of the cabinet are two sides, a top and bottom, and a back panel. These are joined together in such a way that they form a completely

Cutting List

Top: one of 22½ × 10⅝ × ¾in (572 × 270 × 19mm)

Bottom: one of 22½ × 10⅝ × ¾in (572 × 270 × 19mm)

Side: two of 27 × 10⅝ × ¾in (686 × 270 × 19mm)

Back panel: one of 26¼ × 21¾ × ¾in (667 × 552 × 19mm)

Door: two of 25⅜ × 10⅜ × ¾in (645 × 263 × 19mm)

Door cross-piece: four of 10⅜ × 3 × ½in (263 × 76 × 13mm)

Top rail: one of 21 × 5⅛ × ¾in (534 × 130 × 19mm)

Mid rail: one of 19½ × 5⅛ × ¾in (495 × 130 × 19mm)

Bottom rail: one of 21 × 5⅛ × ¾in (534 × 130 × 19mm)

Upright: two of 10 × 5⅛ × ¾in (254 × 130 × 19mm)

Drawer front: one of 19⅜ × 3¾ × ⅝in (492 × 95 × 16mm)

Drawer back: one of 19⅜ × 3¾ × ⅝in (492 × 95 × 16mm)

Drawer side :   two of 3⅞ × 3¾ × ⅝in (98 × 95 × 16mm)

Drawer bottom: one of 18½ × 4¼ × ¼in (470 × 108 × 6mm)

Chisel rack: one of 8 × 1¾ × ⅞in (203 × 45 × 22mm)

rigid structure, to which the two doors are attached and into which the interior shelves are fitted. The shelves are purposely built as a separate and detachable unit so that you can make alterations at a later stage.

The external dimensions are governed, to a certain extent, by the material from which the cabinet is made. There is little point in spending a lot of money on expensive timber, and the most reasonable choice is whitewood. Each panel is built up from lengths of 5¾ × ¾in (145 × 19mm) tongued-and-grooved material: two lengths jointed edge to edge for each of the top, bottom, side and door panels, and four lengths for the back panel.

Mark all the boards to the required length, adding an extra 1in (25mm) as a safety margin, and cut them into individual pieces with the saw. Fit them together in pairs for the top, bottom, side and door panels, and a row of four for the back panel, arranging them so that the growth rings that are visible on the end-grain go in alternating directions. Slot the tongue into the groove to check that the joints all fit perfectly.

Plane off the tongue and the groove from the two outer edges, taking each pair of boards to a width of 10⅝in (270mm) for the top, bottom and side panels, and 10⅜in (264mm) for the two doors, and planing the edges of the two outermost boards that make up the back panel so that it is 21⅝in (550mm) wide overall.

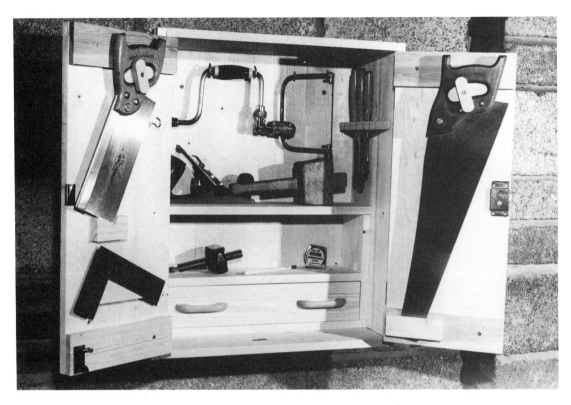

The tool cabinet should be built to house most of the tools you are likely to need, possibly leaving room for later acquisitions. Note that the insides of the two doors are used to advantage. Large power tools will have to be stored elsewhere.

Mix a quantity of wood glue and apply it to the tongues and grooves with a small brush, assembling all the joints and holding them tightly together with cramps while the glue dries and hardens. Wipe away any excess glue which may have squeezed out from the assembled joints, with a damp cloth, before it sets.

Measure the top, bottom and side panels to their exact length, square across at each end and cut off the small amount of waste using the handsaw. The top and bottom panels are fitted to the two side panels with bridle joints, which are alternatively known as slot mortise and tenon joints. These bear a strong resemblance to the dovetail joint, but they are easier and quicker to cut. As with the conventional bridle, or mortise and tenon, the pins are clearly defined, but the mortise equivalents amount to no more than a series of slots at the end of the board into which the pins fit.

Make a card template with slots and pins marked, and cut in an alternating pattern, arranging for these to be of equal thickness, starting with a pin, then a slot, and so on until you finish at the opposite edge with a pin. These should fit exactly within the width of the board which, at 10⅝in (270mm), means that the most convenient number of individual segments is nine, each having a width of 1³⁄₁₆in (30mm).

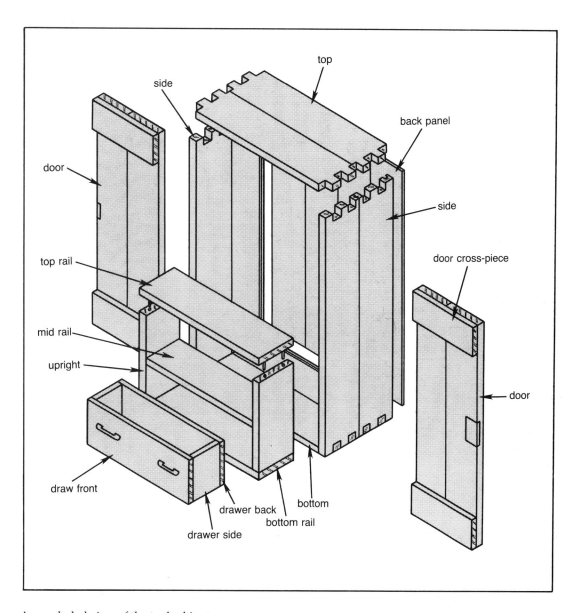

An exploded view of the tool cabinet.

Use the template to mark the pattern at each end of the four boards, and cut out the waste from between the pencilled lines with the tenon saw and the chisel, so that where two boards meet to form a right-angled corner joint, the two parts interlock with the pins entering the slots. When all four corners are complete, make a trial assembly at the top, bottom and side panels to check that they all fit perfectly together.

The back panel is located with housing joints, consisting of a tongue cut along all four edges which fits into a groove cut on the inside face of the four main panels. As the boards from which the back panel is made are ¾in (19mm) thick, the tongues and grooves are each set to a width of ⅜in (9mm) and placed at a distance of ⅜in (9mm) from the rear edge of the four panels.

Lay the cabinet on top of the back panel, testing the four corners with the square and adjusting if necessary until they are all at perfect right-angles, then mark around the four edges in pencil inside the cabinet, leaving four lines on the back panel. Assuming that the cabinet has been accurately centralised on the back panel, this should leave an extra ⅜in (9mm) to form the tongue along each edge. Set the depth of the waste to ⅜in (9mm), marking with the gauge.

Set the mortise gauge to mark the grooves, and scribe two parallel lines along each of the inside faces of the top, bottom and side panels, having firstly dismantled the assembly. Clamp these, one at a time, to the side of the workbench and cut the grooves with the plough plane to a depth of ⅜in (9mm). An alternative tool for this job is the electric router.

There are several ways of cutting the tongue around the four edges of the back panel. The quickest and simplest method is to use the router, but if you do not yet possess one, the plough plane is a good option, although one difficulty can arise here, since the plough requires a special attachment before it can cut across the grain. The third method is to take a length of straight-edged hardwood batten and clamp it along each of the waste lines drawn on the back panel, one at a time, so that it provides a guide for the tenon saw. Work the saw back and forth along the wooden guide until you have cut to the required depth of ⅜in (9mm). In this instance, it is easier to make the cut across the grain than it is along it, due to the fact that the blade of

the tenon saw is more effective working at an angle to the direction of the grain, a feature which is always encountered in woodwork.

When you have sawn to the indicated depth, cut along the scribed depth line with a wide-bladed chisel and mallet to remove the waste, leaving a neat tongue. Assemble the back panel to the four main panels of the cabinet, and knock all the joints fully together with the mallet, checking that each of the four corners meets perfectly. Once you are satisfied with the result, dismantle the five component parts, mix more wood glue, and brush this well into each joint, cramping up the cabinet assembly.

Trim the doors to length and if necessary plane them down until they fit side-by-side within the cabinet. Cut the two strengthening cross-pieces for each door, one at the top and one at the bottom, and drill them with two countersunk number 8 screw holes each, to take 1in (25mm) woodscrews. Glue and screw the cross-pieces in place.

The inside surfaces of both doors are used to house the handsaw, tenon saw, square and any other flat tool that can be hung easily. Both saws are held in place by gluing a shaped wooden block along the bottom edge of the top cross-piece corresponding to the shape of the saw's handgrip opening, with a rounded wooden retaining peg cut from 1 × ½in (25 × 13mm) hardwood and screwed on in such a fashion that it can revolve to hold the saw handgrip against the door, or turn through 90 degrees to release it.

The blade of the handsaw is held in place within a slot cut in a piece of scrap wood which is glued to the bottom cross-piece, and the bottom of the tenon saw rests in a notch cut in a piece that is stuck

Specially shaped saw retainers are cut to the exact contours of the opening in the handgrip of the handsaw and tenon saw, and glued to the top inside surface of each door.

in an appropriate position on the inside of the door itself. Other blocks of wood may be specially cut to hold the square and similar tools, if space permits.

Attach the doors to the cabinet with two 2in (50mm) butt hinges each, cutting shallow rebates in the edges of the doors and the inside surface of the two sides. Fit the hinges in place with ½in (13mm) number 6 woodscrews. The left-hand door is held in the closed position with a simple drop bolt, and the right-hand door is given a cabinet-type door lock, complete with brass escutcheon.

The interior shelving and drawer arrangement is made from planed white-wood, with the top and bottom shelves cut so that they just fit between the two sides, the uprights dowel-jointed to them and an intermediate shelf joined like-wise, leaving enough space beneath it to fit the small drawer.

The drawer is constructed from a front, a back and two side panels, each with a shallow groove cut close to the bottom edge to receive a piece of ¼in (6mm)-thick plywood for the bottom. The various main components of the drawer are dowel-jointed together, using ¼in (6mm)-diameter dowelling, and the front panel finished off by fitting two long wooden drawer handles.

The chisel rack is made from a piece of 1¾ × ¾in (45 × 19mm) wood, which has a row of ¾in (19mm) diameter and ⅝in (16mm) diameter holes drilled right through its thickness, with narrow openings cut by sawing out notches, so that the chisel blades can be slotted in and seated on their brass collars. The rack is fixed to the inside of the cabinet with two dowels and glue.

Other tools, like the handbrace, can be stored on hooks screwed into the back panel. Drill bits may be arranged in order of size in a block of wood which has corresponding-sized holes bored in a row to receive them.

The cabinet will probably look at its best if it remains in a natural wood finish. Be sure to treat it thoroughly with pre-servative before applying a clear poly-urethane varnish.

Finally, attach it to the wall of the workshop by drilling four holes in the back panel, one in every corner; then hold the cabinet against the wall, with a spirit level placed against it to ensure that the sides are vertical, and mark the hole positions in the brickwork of the garage, or the timber-clad wall of the garden shed. Prepare the holes, and fit the cabinet in place with 2in (50mm) number 10 woodscrews.

2 Tools for the Job

When you have found somewhere convenient to work, the next step is to start building up a collection of good woodworking tools. No doubt you will already possess a few items – most of us accumulate a variety of tools over the years – but what you must remember is that only the best will do. What is the use of devoting precious time and money to the task of making your own furniture if the tools are not up to the job?

First, you must be prepared to set aside a sum of money for purchasing the most essential tools. Make a point of buying well-known brand names which can be relied upon for their high quality and long working life. Do not invest in cheap tools, because they are invariably a false economy.

Exactly what items, and how many, you decide to buy will clearly depend on the range of tools that you require for your chosen line of work, and how much you can afford to spend at any one time. You will soon find that you can never have enough tools at your disposal, so this ought to solve all future problems as to what gifts you should receive for Christmas and birthdays!

There are, of course, a number of tools which must be regarded as absolutely essential if you are to produce top-quality results. Some of these might appear at first sight to duplicate the function of others, but they all have their own special purpose and it is usually a mistake to attempt an action for which the tool was not intended. There are exceptions to this rule, as you will find out in due course. But for the moment, let us consider the type of tools that you should aim to include in your tool cabinet.

MEASURING TOOLS

All cabinet-making depends for its success on accurate measurement, and the rule or tape is probably used more than any other single tool. My own choice is the spring-loaded flexible steel tape-measure which pulls out from a metal casing, has a lock to hold it in any position, and retracts back into the casing when not in use. The scale is marked on one face in inches and centimetres. An L-shaped steel lip is attached to the free end of the tape, and serves to mark the zero position; it hooks easily over the edge of the wood for this purpose, and also prevents the tape from vanishing completely into the case. This particular variety of tape-measure can be obtained with a capacity of 2m or 3m when it is fully extended – in fact, some models go even further – and this means that long lengths of wood can be measured in a single movement.

An alternative measuring tool is the traditional carpenter's wooden rule, which is designed so that it folds up into four equal segments. The usual length for the rule is 2ft, so it has become known as the 24-inch gauge.

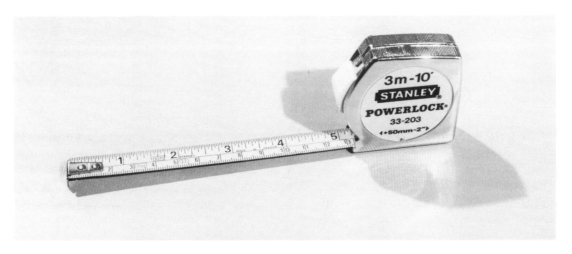

The retractable steel tape-measure is recommended for general use. Various maximum lengths are available, and the 3m model will probably prove the most versatile. Measurements are marked in imperial inches and metric millimetres.

The most important feature of your tape-measure or rule is that it must be calibrated in imperial and metric measurements – but always take care not to mix them up. For example, it is never a good idea to start working in inches and then convert to millimetres in the middle of a project. There will always be a slight difference between the two systems, and in high-class furniture-making you have little room for error.

MARKING TOOLS

The Pencil You might think that there are already enough pencils lying around the house without having to buy one especially for woodwork. I normally use an ordinary HB pencil which I keep well sharpened to retain a fine point, but if you care to you can purchase a carpenter's pencil which is oval in cross-section and is perhaps easier to grip.

Do not use a pencil with a hard lead, because this will score the surface of the wood and the marks may prove difficult to remove later at the sandpapering stage. Neither do you want a very soft lead, since this quickly loses its fine point and you end up drawing thick lines. An HB lead is a good compromise.

The Marking Knife This is used when the marking calls for a thin line to be scribed on the surface of the wood, as in the case of marking out the sockets for a dovetail joint, or going over a previously-squared pencil line so that a sloped chisel cut can be made to create a channel for the saw to start its cut in the preparation of many joints. The Stanley knife is ideal, because it has a handle that fits easily into the palm of the hand and a guard to fit over the blade when not in use. Other similar types of knife have a retractable blade. Spare blades can be bought in packets, and are easy to replace.

The Bradawl This is a marking tool which has a handle shaped rather like that of a screwdriver, and is fitted with a short steel spike which terminates in a sharp point. Some bradawls are square in section, whilst others have a cylindrical spike. The square version allows the spike to be withdrawn more easily from the wood once it has been twisted back and forth. The purpose of the bradawl is to start off screw holes and help to prevent the wood from splitting.

The Square When marking wood, it is usual practice to draw a line at right-angles to its length. The square consists of a rectangular wooden handle, edged in brass, which has a steel blade attached to it at 90 degrees with two parallel edges.

The Mitre Square A somewhat more sophisticated version of the ordinary square, the mitre square has an adjustable blade which can be set at any angle between 45 degrees and 90 degrees, and is of all-metal construction. A simpler type has a wooden handle and a blade which is fixed at 45 degrees.

The Marking Gauge This tool, used for scribing a single line along a piece of wood, has a wooden stock, in which a hardened steel spur is mounted at one end, and a sliding wooden fence which can be locked in any position. Strictly speaking, the marking gauge is designed to mark lines that run in the same direction as the wood grain. For marking across the grain, a slightly different tool called a cutting gauge is used, which has a sharp steel blade instead of a spur, to cut through the fibres of the wood without tearing or snatching. However, with care the marking gauge can be used for both occasions.

The Mortise Gauge Similar in appearance to the marking gauge, the mortise gauge differs in that it has two spurs, one of which is adjustable, so that two parallel lines can be marked on the wood. The best types of mortise gauge are equipped with a rounded brass thumbscrew at the opposite end from the spurs, to control

A pencil, square, knife and mortise gauge are the tools principally employed for marking the wood. Some mortise gauges are also equipped with a single spur, allowing them to be used as a marking gauge as well.

26

the position of the inner moveable spur with great precision. As with the marking gauge, the wooden fence is released and tightened by means of a screw.

Most mortise gauges combine two functions by having double spurs on one side of the stock to mark mortises, and a single spur on the opposite side to provide a marking facility.

SAWS

The Handsaw This is a general-purpose saw which you will use to do most of your preparatory cutting. It normally measures around 24in (610mm) in length, and has either eight or ten teeth to the inch, although some have as few as six. The teeth are set in an alternating pattern so that as the saw cuts into the wood it creates a passage known as the kerf which is wider than the thickness of the blade, thus ensuring that it does not bind or jam. Some handsaws have blades with a straight back, but the skew-backed blade is more popular. This type of saw is designed for cutting at right-angles to the direction of the grain, though in practice it is often called upon to cut with the grain also.

Another version of the handsaw is one in which the teeth are all raked back at an angle and there is no alternative setting. This type is known as the rip saw, and is intended only for cutting in the same direction as the grain. The rip saw has a very limited use in the realms of cabinet-making, and a good handsaw is recommended for all preliminary cutting.

Handsaws are available with either wooden or plastic handgrips, and the choice is a matter of personal preference. Plastic is lighter and perhaps makes the

task of sawing less arduous, but a wooden handgrip gives a firmer hold and the extra weight enables you to give a heavier cut. For that reason, it is still very much favoured by traditional woodworkers. Whichever sort of handgrip is fitted to the saw, the correct method of holding it is to have the forefinger of your hand pointing forward in the same direction as the blade.

The Tenon Saw As its name suggests, the tenon saw is mostly used for cutting tenons and other types of joint. It is shorter than the handsaw, and has between twelve and twenty teeth to the inch. The top edge of the blade is strengthened with a steel or brass back to give rigidity and ensure a straight cut, and for that reason it is also known as the backsaw. The teeth are given an alternating set, as with the handsaw, but this is less pronounced in appearance. The blade length ranges from 8in (200mm) to 12in (305mm). Once again, a wooden handgrip is an advantage.

The Coping Saw A very useful saw when you need to cut curves. The thin blade is mounted in a metal frame shaped in the form of a U, and held under tension by tightening the handgrip. If the handgrip is slackened off, the blade can be rotated about its axis within the frame to set it at any desired angle.

The teeth of the blade are rather coarse compared with the hacksaw, and the blade can be removed from the frame when it gets worn, and changed for another. As the coping saw has this facility, it can be used to cut internal holes within the wood by firstly drilling through the piece with the brace and bit, inserting the free end of the blade, then

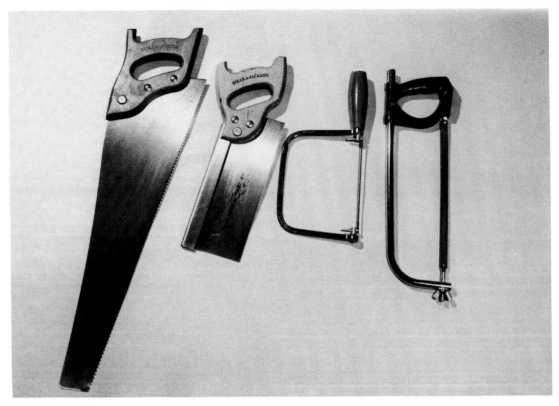

For cutting the wood, you will need a tenon saw and coping saw, and occasionally a hacksaw.

re-attaching it to the frame before commencing the cut.

The Hacksaw At first sight, the hacksaw bears a close resemblance to the coping saw, because the blade is held in a metal frame and can be changed. But the teeth are much finer, as already stated, and the blade cannot be rotated. The hacksaw is mostly used for cutting metal, although it is equally useful for sawing hardwood dowel material, when the fineness of the blade makes for a smooth, light cut.

The Jigsaw In its most common form, this is a hand-held power tool in which the saw blade oscillates up and down at very high speed to provide a fast and highly manoeuvrable means of cutting. Some of the more expensive models have a range of speed settings, and a knob may be provided to turn the blade. There are many occasions when the jigsaw is an invaluable tool, but having said that, it does no more than any of the foregoing saws, except that it reduces the amount of physical effort and produces a quicker result.

Saw Maintenance

All saws must be carefully looked after, if they are to give you years of reliable service. Handsaws and tenon saws have their blades correctly set and fully sharpened when you buy them – but inevitably they wear after prolonged use. The blunting effect of certain hardwoods only hastens the process. Check the teeth regularly, and at the first sign of wear arrange for the blade to be re-sharpened. You can obtain special sharpening tools to do the job yourself, but the better course of action is to take the saw to your local tool dealer and ask for the teeth to be sharpened and re-set by a specialist.

The blades of the coping saw, hacksaw and jigsaw are detachable, so the task of keeping them sharp is simply a matter of taking off the old blunt saw blade and replacing it with a new one. Sets of blades are available in packets, and jigsaw blades come in a wide range of teeth sizes and pitches.

Maintenance of the electrically-powered jigsaw is confined to the periodical changing of the motor's brushes. Anything other than that will require expert attention.

CHISELS

It is advisable to have a set of chisels covering a range of sizes so that you can select the most suitable width of blade for the job in hand. There are various types of chisel, and each has its own particular characteristics.

The Firmer Chisel The firmer chisel has a strong cutting blade with square edges, and the appearance of being a robust tool capable of standing up to sustained heavy use. Typical blade widths are ¼in (6mm), ⅜in (9mm), ½in (13mm), ⅝in (16mm), ¾in (19mm), ⅞in (22mm) and

1in (25mm). The handle may be made from wood or plastic. As the firmer chisel is intended to be used for chopping out wood, the handle is always large enough to be easily grasped with one hand while the end is struck a series of heavy blows with a wooden mallet. Never hit the chisel with a hammer.

The Bevelled Chisel The bevelled chisel, in which the two edges of the blade are sloped, makes the tool ideal for cutting dovetail joints, because the angle of the two bevels permits the chisel to work inside the dovetails. Indeed, the bevelled chisel has a much wider application because the steel from which the blade is forged has such strength that it can be employed for most cutting tasks, including the chopping out of mortises in cabinet work.

Bevelled chisels are available in the same range of blade widths as the firmer chisel. Where most of your cutting work is restricted to the preparing of cabinet

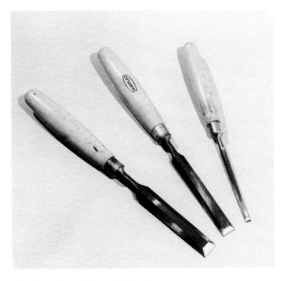

A selection of bevel chisels.

29

joints, you are advised to purchase a full set of bevelled chisels and use these for all your chopping and paring operations.

The Mortise Chisel The final example is the mortise chisel, which has a thick blade designed to resist any tendency to bend when cutting large deep mortises, where great pressure is exerted. It is designed for heavy-duty work, in which the blade is not only used to cut down into the joint but also to lever out the waste. The sides of the blade are usually given a slight taper towards the tip of the cutting edge, to prevent the chisel from jamming in the workpiece.

There are few occasions, if any, when the mortise chisel is needed for furniture-making, and therefore this tool is not vital.

Sharpening the Chisel

From time to time, the cutting edge of your chisels will start to feel rather blunt, especially when they are used to cut some of the denser hardwoods. Sharpening a chisel is one of the most basic and routine jobs that the serious woodworker must undertake, for it is most unwise to persist in using the tool once the cutting tip has gone dull and lifeless.

Sharpening is carried out on an oilstone, which is a flat, rectangular block of material with two abrasive faces. One face is coarse, the other fine. Most tool sharpening can be done on the fine surface. To use the stone, begin by placing it on a level surface where it will not slip – either by resting one end against the bench stop, or placing it in the tool tray – and add several drops of thin oil. Pick up the chisel and examine the tip of the blade. You will see that there are two

distinct angles. The first of these is the main bevel (not to be confused with the bevel running along the two edges of the bevelled chisel) which forms a comparatively shallow angle with the flat underside of the blade; and the second bevel is worked along the tip to create the honed cutting edge.

Present the chisel to the oilstone so that the flat underside is facing uppermost, with the main bevel resting fully on the stone. Note that the handle and blade form an angle of approximately 30 degrees with the surface of the stone. Work the chisel back and forth, keeping the handle at a constant angle, to grind a new face on the bevel. Take care not to rub on one part of the stone only, otherwise you will eventually form a dip. Work the blade over the entire surface, applying fresh oil when necessary.

The fine cutting tip is applied by rais-

The blade of the chisel is sharpened on an oilstone.

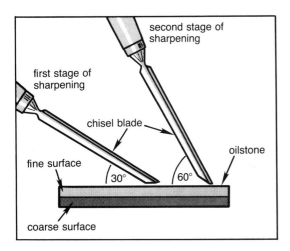

Sharpening a chisel blade.

ing the handle of the chisel to increase the angle. The actual amount can only be judged with practice, but as a rule it is safe to say that a firmer chisel can be given a deeper cutting tip than the bevelled chisel. Aim for between 50 and 60 degrees.

Once the honing of the tip has been completed, there will be a small amount of burring present, known as a wire edge, which must be removed by reversing the blade, laying it flat on the oilstone and drawing it back towards you once or twice. Carefully rub the end of the blade with a soft cloth to get rid of all traces of oil, remembering to keep your fingers well away from the sharp edge. Finally, clean the stone with white spirit, dry it with a rag and put it away until it is needed next time.

Chisels made by reputable manufacturers will last a long time, provided they are treated with respect. This means that the handle must never be struck with anything other than a good-quality wooden mallet, and the blade used solely for the purpose of cutting wood.

GOUGES

These are specialised tools which superficially resemble the chisel, and are used mainly for cutting out grooves, or paring curved surfaces. There are two main types. One has a concave blade, with the cutting bevel prepared on the inside of the blade; it is known as an *in cannel*. The other, also with a concave blade, has the cutting bevel on the outside, and is known as an *out cannel*.

Although, like chisels, gouges can be obtained in a range of sizes, their use is somewhat restricted. If you feel inclined to purchase a pair of gouges, settle for a size of ½in (13mm) as this will undoubtedly prove to be the most versatile.

PLANES

The Smoothing Plane This is the most frequently used bench plane, and as far as our work is concerned, the best choice for cabinet work. There are other types of bench plane available, namely the much larger jack plane, but this particular tool is intended for the preparatory planing of rough timber and is only an asset if you purchase your wood in the sawn rather than the prepared state.

The usual choice of smoothing plane is made from steel, fitted with either a wooden or plastic handle and knob. The cutter blade is easily detachable for sharpening and, when installed against the backiron, is provided with a lateral adjustment lever. The thickness of shaving is altered by turning the brass adjusting nut, and it is usual to set the blade so that when viewed along the sole, the cutting tip appears no thicker than a hair's breadth.

The Bullnose Rebate Plane This is a smaller type of plane which is especially useful to the cabinet-maker because it has the blade mounted in a forward position from where it can reach deep into tight corners. For this reason, it has many more applications than merely cutting out rebates. The bullnose plane is not an essential tool for the amateur woodworker, but it is certainly desirable.

The Plough Plane Also known as the combination plane, this tool is of an even more specialised nature than the bullnose plane. It consists of a cast iron body to which the blade is attached, together with the handle. Two parallel steel rods protrude sideways from the body of the plane and carry the adjustable cast iron fence. There is a depth guide which can be raised or lowered to suit the nature of the cut. A range of cutters can be fitted to the plough plane, providing a wide variety of operations: grooving, filleting, reeding, rebating and preparing edge mouldings. It is a highly versatile tool.

The Electric Plane A high-speed tool which does much the same work as the smoothing plane, except that the physical effort is reduced and the task of planing down the wood made a lot quicker. The planing action is facilitated by a revolving drum which carries two identical blades, placed 180 degrees apart. As the drum spins at speeds of up to 20,000 rpm, the blades alternately come into contact with the surface of the wood and remove small amounts as the plane is pushed forward. There is a knob for altering the depth, which works by raising or lowering the sole at the front whilst the position of the spinning drum remains constant.

Maintenance of the electric plane is limited to replacing the blades when they wear down. Their blunted cutting edges cannot be re-sharpened, but the working life is prolonged by the simple expedient of providing each blade with a double edge. In time, the toothed rubber drive belt will probably break, but its replacement is an easy task. However, one word of caution regarding this tool: no matter how much the electric plane speeds up the job and cuts down the amount of time and effort on what might seem a somewhat mundane process, it must not be permitted to take over completely from the equivalent hand tool. The finest results still rely on the feel of the smoothing plane's blade cutting crisply along the grain, and being transmitted back to the woodworker's hands.

The Spokeshave This is the last type of plane in common use, and as its name implies, is has a connection with the time-honoured craft of the wheelwright. Its function is mainly to shape curved surfaces. The body is usually made from malleable iron and is provided with two projecting wings, each of which is grasped by the fingers of one hand to exert firm and even pressure. The blade is held in place with a plate, and two knurled wheels can be turned on threaded shafts to move the blade back and forth, thus increasing or decreasing the depth of the cut, resulting in a coarse or fine wood shaving.

The spokeshave is available in two models, one with a convex curve, and the other a concave curve. In either case, plenty of practice is needed before the tool can be used to good effect.

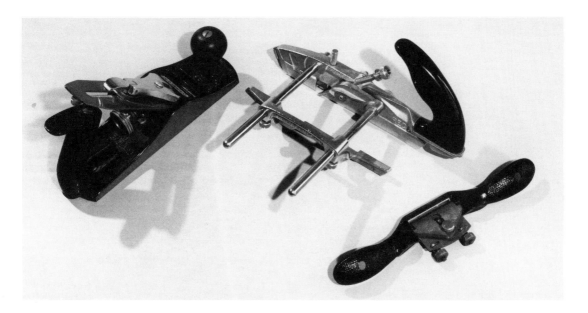

Most hand-planing operations can be left to the smoothing plane, plough plane and spokeshave.

Maintenance of Planes

As with the chisel, the blade of the smoothing plane, the plough plane, the bullnose rebate plane and the spokeshave, all require re-sharpening occasionally, using the oilstone method. Sometimes, when the cutting edge is badly dulled, the blade will need to have a new bevel applied using a special grinding machine, and this is a service which your local tool dealer should be able to provide.

DRILLS

The Brace Drill This tool is used for the majority of drilling operations. It consists of a crank forged from steel which is fitted with a rounded wooden or plastic handle at one end and a chuck at the other, for holding a variety of drill bits. When choosing a brace, opt for one that has a ratchet movement because this is invaluable when working in tight corners. The jaws of the chuck are tightened and loosened by gripping the outer shank, which has a knurled surface, and turning it.

The Hand Drill A more compact type of drill than the brace, the hand drill does not have a crank, but the motive power is supplied by turning a wheel which is set midway along the frame and geared to two pinions which turn the chuck. The drilling action is firm and positive, but does not provide the same amount of torque, or turning effect, as the brace. The hand drill is therefore more suited to light drilling work. Some chuck designs need a special key to be inserted into the toothed rim for tightening and loosening, as with a power drill.

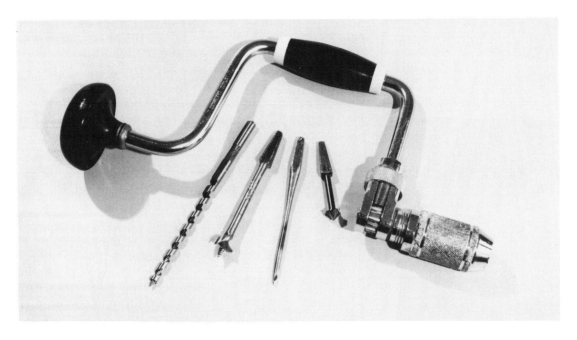

The ratchet handbrace is designed to accept a range of drill bits. Shown from left to right: ¼in (6mm)-diameter auger bit, ⅝in (16mm)-diameter centre bit, number 8 wood bit, and a rosehead countersink.

The Electric Drill   The hand-held electric drill is now universally accepted as the most suitable for most drilling jobs. Some of the more expensive models are even provided with variable speed operation. However, whilst this tool certainly has its place in woodwork, we must bear in mind that the cabinet-maker is more concerned with doing the job slowly by hand, with precision. If the power drill is to have a role to play on the workbench, it should be used in conjunction with a drill stand to ensure maximum accuracy.

Drill Bits

These provide your drill with its cutting edge. Those used in the brace are square-tanged so that they can be gripped by the chuck, but power drills usually only accept bits that have round shanks. The hand drill, depending on the type of chuck fitted, will take either one or the other.

For most woodworking purposes, a useful range of bits would be: for boring screw holes, the appropriate size of woodscrew bit, such as a number 8 or number 10; for dowel holes, and drilling out the first stage of a mortise, a selection of centre bits such as ⅜in (9mm), ½in (13mm), ⅝in (16mm), ¾in (19mm), ⅞in (22mm) and 1in (25mm). Larger diameter holes will need an adjustable expansive bit, which is very much like the centre bit in appearance, but has a sliding cutter that can be fixed in a number of positions.

Long spiral-shaped auger bits have a long reach and are useful for drilling deep into the wood, particularly for boring a straight line into end-grain; and a rosehead countersink is needed for screws so that their heads can be recessed to lie flush with the surface of the wood. You will occasionally find it convenient to use a small-diameter twist drill, which can also be used for boring into metal, and this is usually mounted in the chuck of a hand drill or power drill.

There are times when you are called upon to drill a hole to a pre-determined depth with great accuracy. Certain types of bit are provided with a sliding plastic collar which acts as a depth guide, but the shape of the centre bit makes this impossible. However, you can easily make your own depth gauge by sticking a short length of self-adhesive tape to the shaft of the bit in a position that coincides with the required depth. Always use this method instead of guesswork. Drill stands have their own scales set behind the operating lever, and are pre-set against an automatic stop which prevents the entire drill from travelling further than you intend.

One last word about drill bits: in cabinet-making, the majority of drilling operations are carried out at right-angles to the direction of the wood grain; but there are occasions when the bit must be cut into the end-grain. There can be a problem when using a centre bit, because it has a habit of drifting out of line as it cuts into the wood, following the path of least resistance within the grain. For end-grain drilling, it is important to use either a twist drill or an auger, both of which have a continuous spiral pattern along the length of the bit, keeping the cutting action running in a straight line.

THE ELECTRIC ROUTER

This probably counts as the most specialised tool that the amateur furniture-maker is likely to buy, and it is well worth setting enough money aside to purchase a good one. There is always an element of mystery about a tool which has a reputation for performing many functions, in this case rebating, edge-moulding, grooving and fluting, to name but a few.

In fact, the electric router is simply a motor housed vertically inside the body of the tool, which drives a chuck at very high revolutions. Into the chuck may be fitted a wide range of cutters. These include straight cutters for making rebates, housing grooves and mortises; Roman ogee and corner round cutters for working edge-moulding patterns; and semi-circular cutters for fluting.

Because the cutter turns at such a high speed, it produces a very clean cut regardless of whether the router is moved along in the same direction as the grain or at right-angles to it, making this tool more versatile than the plough plane. The base of the router is circular, so that it can be lined up beside a length of straight-edged batten, acting as its guide, and steered through any angle without deviating from a straight path. A detachable fence can be mounted beneath the base to provide the router with its own adjustable guide, and the spring-loaded plunging action of the body may be pre-set against a scaled depth stop so that the cutter is accurately controlled both laterally and vertically.

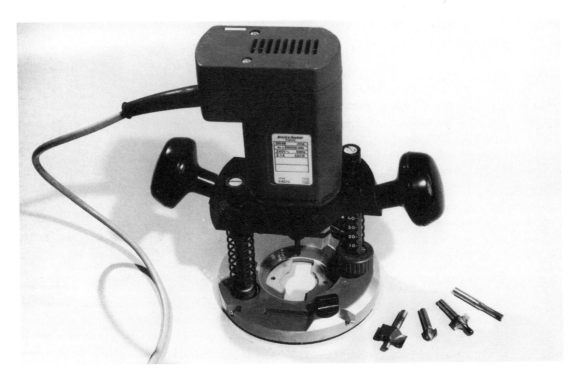

The electric router, with various cutters.

HAMMERS

The Wooden Mallet Although it does not count as a hammer in the true sense of the word, the mallet is used whenever a blow needs to be struck in the course of cutting joints and assembling the work – with the exception of driving in nails. The mallet's large head is made from beech, and the handle, which is wedge-shaped to prevent the head from flying off, is often cut from ash. Both materials are very hard and durable.

The Hammer It is a good idea to have two sizes of hammer, one a rather heavy type with a claw for extracting unwanted nails, and the other a light joiner's hammer for knocking in small nails and veneer pins. The heads are forged from steel, and the handles made from ash. Most households already own a hammer of some description, and as the tool is seldom used in furniture-making, you might be tempted to make do with what you have already got. Nevertheless, a lightweight tack hammer is a good investment.

SCREWDRIVERS

As in the case of the chisel, there is no single size of screwdriver which can be said to serve all purposes adequately. For one thing, there are two basic types of screw: there is the traditional slot-head screw, which has a single slot cut across the diameter of its head, and there is the cross-head screw, in which two slots are

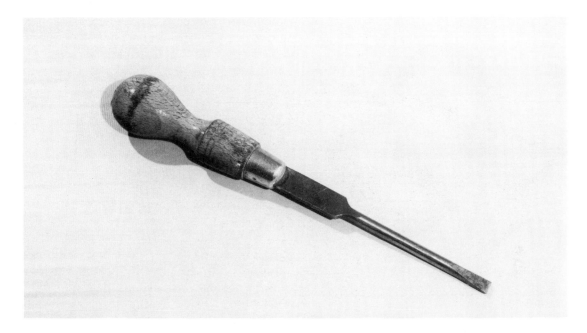

As only single slot screws are recommended for use in high-quality cabinet-making, only one type of screwdriver need be considered, the cabinet screwdriver. It is fitted with a large, bulbous wooden handle which is easy to grasp.

arranged in the form of a cross and set into the head without reaching the circumference. The latter often has a double thread, and is a popular choice for composite materials like chipboard.

For the cabinet-maker who wishes to indulge a passion for building high-class reproduction-style furniture, or contemporary designs with a superior quality and top-grade finish, the choice will undoubtedly be that of the slot-head screw. The correct tool in this instance is the cabinet screwdriver, which has a rather old-fashioned appearance, with a large oval-shaped and bulbous handle. The blade is made from an alloy of steel, giving it great strength, and the tip is flared outwards so that it fits completely into the screw slot. Various sizes of screwdriver are available, to suit the wide range of screws.

Since no other type of screw need be used, a good investment would be to purchase a small, medium and large slot-head cabinet screwdriver. If financial considerations curb your natural zeal to buy the lot, then the best economy is to settle for the medium size.

CLAMPS AND CRAMPS

The G-Clamp The G-clamp is so named although the frame of the clamp is shaped in the form of the letter C, as it becomes a 'G' when the adjustable screw is taken into account. A pair of G-clamps are very useful for holding pieces of wood to the side of the workbench, as has been previously mentioned. There are many sizes available, but the cabinet-maker does not need anything too large or heavy. Varia-

37

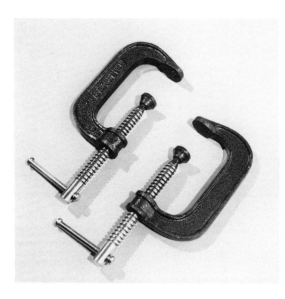

A pair of G-clamps.

The Sash Cramp This device consists of a long steel bar in which a series of holes has been drilled at regular intervals. At one end, a cast iron head is fixed, and this has an adjustable screw action somewhat like that of the vice, which bears upon a moveable slide. Further along the bar, a second slide equipped with a detachable retaining pin can be set in any position where the pin can be passed through one of the holes.

The cramp is used to apply pressure to the assembled workpiece while the glue is drying, and it is standard practice to have at least two of these implements, and often three, bearing upon the assembly. However, sash cramps are quite expensive, and will, therefore, require a relatively large financial outlay. It is a good idea to look through the columns of second-hand goods for sale in your local newspaper, as they do sometimes appear there.

tions on the design include the deep throat clamp, which has a longer reach than the ordinary G-clamp; and the edging clamp which is provided with a second screw thread working at right-angles to the main screw action, to hold edging strips in place during assembly.

The String Tourniquet In the absence of a set of sash cramps, it is possible to

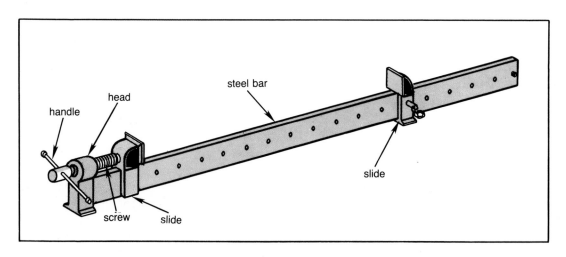

The sash cramp.

apply great pressure to an assembled piece of work by tying a length of strong nylon string around the joints and twisting with a long bar, such as the shaft of a screwdriver, to apply a tourniquet. You must be careful, if you use this method, to place some scrap wood between the string and the workpiece, or else the tautened string will cut into the corners and edges, causing noticeable depressions.

ABRASIVE MATERIALS

The File A tool widely used in metalwork, the file has a more limited role as far as the cabinet-maker is concerned. It is used only to erase imperfections and leave a smooth, clean edge in areas where tools such as the plane and spokeshave cannot reach.

The standard shape for the file is flat on both sides, but there are other types which offer a half-round surface, triangular and circular cross-sections, of which the last example is usually referred to as the 'rat-tail' file. They each have an abrasive surface which consists of many rows of tiny teeth, and vary in the degree of roughness. A very coarse type would be unsuitable for the woodworker, because even the hardest of woods yield to the backward and forward rubbing action of a finely-patterned file.

You will notice that one end of the file always comes to a point, known as the tang, and this is the end which you hold. For safety's sake, be sure to fit a wooden handle over the tang, since this will allow you to take a firmer grasp on the tool. It will also prevent the sharp point digging into your palm if the file meets resistance and suddenly stops.

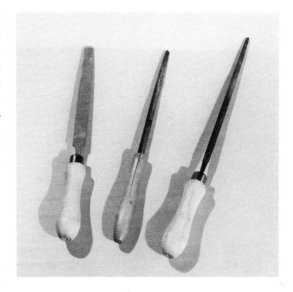

A useful assortment of files should include flat faced, triangular and rat-tail varieties. The sharp tang at the end must always be covered with a wooden handle.

Sandpaper It is hard to imagine making any finished piece of furniture without turning to sandpaper for the final rubbing down before applying the finish to the wood.

Sandpaper, or glass-paper as it was once known, is a sheet of paper material to which an abrasive substance is applied. This abrasive has a gritty feel to it, and is graded according to the degree of coarseness or refinement that you require. Sandpaper is referred to by various numbers – the higher the number, the finer the grit.

Very coarse grades of paper are not considered suitable for cabinet work, because they are far too rough and will only serve to scratch the surface of the wood badly. Medium grades are normally used for the initial stage of rubbing down, to rid the wood of its slight unevenness, and to remove any pencil reference

39

marks that have been used in the building of the workpiece. For the final part of the rubbing down, switch to the finest grade paper, which will leave the wood feeling very smooth to the touch.

The rule that applies to sandpaper, whichever grade you employ, is that it should either be moulded around a block of wood, or around the fingers of one hand, and worked steadily back and forth in the direction of the grain. Never rub sandpaper across the grain, otherwise it will leave tiny lines and ridges which are difficult to remove except by further prolonged rubbing down with the grain.

Wire Wool This is used during the finishing process, for example when a varnish or French polish is applied to the surface of the wood and requires a light rubbing down in between layers. A very fine wire wool has even less abrasiveness than the finest of papers, and when dipped in white spirit it will succeed in removing excess amounts of lacquer or polish before the next layer is applied.

CARING FOR TOOLS

The most effective way of looking after all your woodworking tools is to store them away safely when not in use. If your workplace is in the garage or garden shed, where the atmosphere is likely to be damp, you can safeguard all steel surfaces from rust by giving them a regular rub over with a soft cloth soaked in light oil. The job does not take long, and ensures excellent protection.

As mentioned earlier, attention must be paid to the condition of saw blades, chisels and planes so that their cutting edges are always keen and efficient. An oilstone is an absolute must if you are to re-sharpen the cutting edges of your chisels and planes at the first sign of wear. Drill bits, too, can be filed to restore their cutting ability; however, this is a job which requires great care, otherwise you can make matters worse by ending up with a tip that actually damages the surface of the wood when it should ideally be making a neat, smooth hole.

It is hard to give a fair assessment of power tools without comparing one particular make with another. Broadly speaking, however, they are all prone to the same faults – namely, the burning out of the motor and its brushes. Keep all your work within the capacity of the tool, and take short breaks from time to time so that it can cool down. Repairs are possible, but they can be expensive, and usually leave you wondering how many other conventional tools you could have bought in the meantime with the same money!

3 Choosing Wood

Before you can begin making any piece of furniture, you must decide what type of wood you are going to use. With so many varieties available, the decision is often rather a difficult one. For instance, careful thought must be given to the appearance of the finished piece, and there is the important question of obtaining it in the right quantity and for an acceptable price.

The fact that most of us live reasonably near to a timber yard may not, in itself, be much help. The vast majority of the wood stocked by these merchants falls into the category known as softwood, and nearly all fine cabinet work is made from hardwood. Before going any further, thought should be given to the two terms 'softwood' and hardwood'. The names suggest that hardwoods are tough and durable, whilst softwoods are weaker and more susceptible to breakage; in fact, certain hardwoods are relatively soft, and a few of the softwoods are particularly hard! So obviously the generic name is misleading, for it does not refer to the actual hardness or softness of a particular wood.

There is another reason for establishing the classification. In the colder regions of the world, such as Scandinavia, Canada and Russia, are the huge forests of evergreen coniferous trees that bear needles and cones. These provide us with softwood. In the tropical regions of Africa, Central and South America, and parts of Indonesia, you will only find deciduous trees that shed their leaves each year. These are the hardwood trees. In other parts of the world, including most of Europe, where the climate is, by comparison, far more temperate, the trees are a mixture of the two. There are a few notable exceptions to this classification. The holly tree, for example, is classed as a hardwood, yet keeps its leaves all year.

The difference between softwood and hardwood is not restricted to the simple matter of whether the tree loses its leaves or not as a regular annual event. The structure of the wood is also quite different. As a rule, softwood trees grow quite rapidly and have larger distances between their annual growth rings than hardwoods, though this is not always the case. Hardwoods, on the other hand, generally have a finer grain structure compared with the coarser softwoods, and the texture is usually more refined. Such qualities will only become apparent when you work with many different woods, and learn to appreciate how one type varies from another.

Most of the wood used in furniture-making is of the hardwood variety as this sort possesses the qualities considered most desirable in cabinet work. However, it would be wrong to assume that all pieces of furniture are made from hardwood. Softwoods such as pine have become very popular in what might be referred to as the 'rustic farmhouse style', and they have the advantage of being considerably cheaper to buy.

Typical examples of hardwood and softwood: on the left is a piece of well-figured oak, and on the right, a length of pine.

PROCESSING WOOD

Initial Preparation

Between the time that the tree is felled and the wood is ready to be fashioned on the workbench, it undergoes a number of processes. Firstly, the bark is stripped from the trunk, which is then sawn into boards. This can be done in two ways: either the log is cut right through in slices, giving plain boards, or it is quartered and the boards cut radially. In its uncut form, the trunk consists of heartwood at the centre, and sapwood near to the bark. Heartwood is dense and mature, whereas sapwood is much softer and has less strength. Since the trunk grows out from the centre, it follows that all heartwood was originally sapwood at one time in its existence.

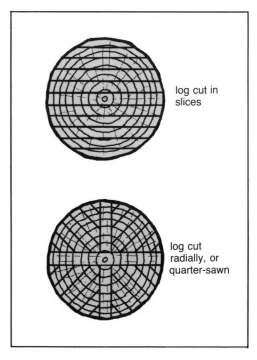

log cut in slices

log cut radially, or quarter-sawn

The two basic methods of sawing the log.

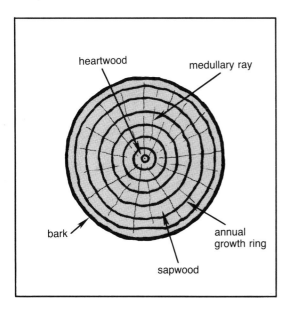

Cross-sectional view of log.

Seasoning

The wood then undergoes a process known as seasoning. This is an essential part of the treatment, in which the sawn boards are stacked and dried so that excess moisture contained within the cells and fibres of the wood can evaporate. If this were not carried out, the timber would be virtually unworkable, and highly susceptible to fungal attack and rot. The two common methods used to dry the wood are air seasoning and kiln drying.

Air Seasoning

This method can take years, and some timber merchants pride themselves on the length of time that their stocks stand out in the open air. The boards are laid carefully in stacks, with skids separating the various layers to provide ventilation. The top of the stack is covered so that the wood is protected from the sun and rain, but the sides are left open for air to circulate freely.

Moisture evaporates from the surfaces of the boards, only to be replaced by water contained deeper in the wood, until eventually the moisture content is uniform throughout. The time taken for this state to be reached depends on the composition of the timber and its thickness. One drawback with this method is that air seasoning does not dry the wood enough for it to be used in the dry atmosphere of centrally-heated houses without the risk of further drying out and the development of splits and cracks. The time and care devoted to the seasoning of timber by this process is rather like the maturing of a fine cognac.

Kiln Drying

The kiln is a large chamber inside which heat is radiated through pipes. A fan artificially controls the air circulation, and in some designs steam can be introduced through special inlets. As with the air seasoning method, the wood is stacked with gaps between each layer. Certain aspects of this process may appear to resemble a Turkish bath! In any event, kiln drying is a technique which ensures that moisture is removed from the wood in a precisely-controlled environment. The time taken for the wood to be treated depends, as with air seasoning, on the initial moisture content, the type and size of the wood, and the extent to which the wood is dried. The kiln drying method is much quicker, all things being equal. However, as far as the cabinet-maker is concerned, it is not nearly as satisfactory.

WOOD SIZES

When the wood has been adequately dried, by whichever method, it is ready to be cut to the size you require. Wood may be ordered in one of two forms, sawn or planed.

Sawn Wood

When cut from the log, and subsequently sawn into smaller sections from the boards, the surface of the wood is rather tough and coarse, and as such is usually only suited to work that remains out of sight. Apart from this, the main characteristic of sawn wood is with regard to its dimensions, for if a particular piece is quoted as being 2 × 1in (50 × 25mm) in cross-section, this is exactly what it should measure.

Planed Wood

Planed wood is also known by the initials PSE (planed square edge) or PAR (planed all round). In contrast to sawn wood, it has its sides and edges prepared from the roughly-sawn state by passing it through a planing machine, which skims off some of the surface to leave a smooth finish. To obtain this result, there must clearly be some reduction in the dimensions of the material, equal to the amount taken off by the plane.

Prepared wood is therefore fractionally smaller in cross-section than its sawn equivalent, and there are two ways in which it may be quoted. For example, the same 2 × 1in (50 × 25mm) piece in the planed form can be referred to either as 2 × 1in (50 × 25mm) prepared, or $1\frac{7}{8}$ × $\frac{7}{8}$in (47 × 22mm) finished size.

When the wood is cut to size from the log, it is said to be sawn, and has a rough feel to its surface (left). After it has been planed, the surface is smooth to the touch and suitable for making into furniture (right).

If you were to specify a measurement of 2 × 1in (50 × 25mm) finished size, the timber merchant would have to prepare it from the next size up in the sawn state, so you will be paying much more for only a little extra material. When you compile your cutting list at the design stage, it makes sense to base all your measurements on the fact that sawn timber is quoted in inches, so that planed wood has fractionally less than the exact inch. The actual amount removed at the planing of the sawn timber varies from one merchant to another.

COMPOSITE MATERIALS

In addition to all the softwoods and hardwoods, there are several other timber products that each have their own particular use. These are plywood, blockboard, chipboard and hardboard. All four types are available in standard sheet sizes, the most common being 8 × 4ft (2,440 × 1,220mm). It is usually possible to purchase smaller sheets.

Plywood is composed of an odd number of thin veneers arranged in such a way that the grain runs in alternating directions, each one being at right-angles to the next. The veneers are bonded to one another under great pressure. The smallest number of veneers is three, but 5-ply and 7-ply are very common. The greater the number of veneers, the thicker is the board and the stronger the plywood.

Blockboard consists of two veneer faces bonded to a core of wood strips, each arranged so that the end-grain alternates in direction. Various thicknesses are available, but the most common is ¾in (19mm).

Chipboard has become one of the most popular materials used in the manufacturing of modern furniture. It is often faced with a wood, plastic or imitation

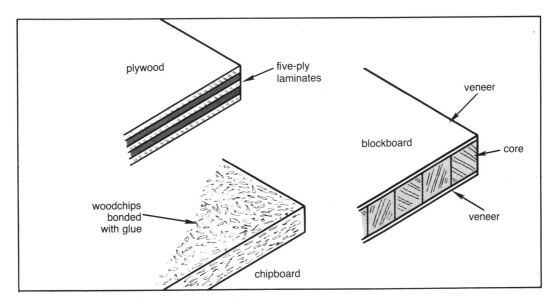

Composite materials.

wood veneer. It is composed of small particles of softwood bonded together with a special resin to form large, flat boards. The standard thickness is ⅝in (16mm). The feature which most distinguishes one type of chipboard from another, apart from the density of the particles and therefore its strength, is the veneer used for the surface finish. It could be teak or mahogany, imitation teak, oak, or coloured melamine.

Hardboard, the last of the composite materials, is made from wood pulp which is compressed into flat boards, usually about ⅛in (4mm) thick. One face is shiny, whilst the other remains rough in texture.

RECOGNITION

When is a piece of wood not a piece of wood? The answer: when it is a piece of chipboard with a layer of plastic imitation wood veneer stuck on top. Sometimes it can be very hard to tell the difference!

At one time, all furniture was made from solid wood; then gradually skilful cabinet-makers discovered that they could use cheaper, rougher wood for the carcase of the furniture, and lay a sheet of high-quality veneer on top. Nobody complained about it, because the carcase was still made from good, solid wood and was constructed with traditional joints which guaranteed that the piece would last a long time and give many years of service. The flourishing antiques trade proves the point. As the years passed by, more concessions were made, and the veneer was laid on a plywood base, which was itself an excellent panelling material owing to its great strength in relation to its thickness.

Now, furniture is largely produced from veneered chipboard, and the nature of this material has significantly changed the structure of the cabinet from a piece of fine craftsmanship to the mass-produced, machine-cut-and-drilled, pre-packed self-assembly unit. It could well be the sense of hopeless frustration that this dreadful modern characterless furniture engenders in the more discerning mind which has persuaded you to seek the assistance of this book.

Natural wood is recognised by its appearance, its weight and its end-grain. Cut the wood with a saw, and you should be able to tell it by the distinctive smell. Oak can be recognised from its unusual and delightful grain pattern and the silver streaks which appear on the surface of radially-sawn boards. Ash and beech also have their own very characteristic appearance, and like oak they are hard to imitate.

Mahogany and teak, on the other hand, may be substituted successfully with other hardwoods such as sapele and afrormosia respectively. There is a difference in the colour of the wood, but the grain pattern is similar. Redwood or pine can be recognised by their knots. These knots have acquired considerable popularity through the making of pine furniture. In moderation, and within the right setting, it can be highly effective.

FAULTS IN WOOD

This brings us very conveniently to the question of faults – because that is what a knot amounts to. It is the point at which a branch joined the trunk of the tree. Provided the knot is live and quite small, it should present no real problem; but

Knotty wood usually causes problems, and as far as possible should be avoided unless the knots are desired for their effect. Most high-quality furniture should be knot-free.

Warping of the wood is caused by uneven drying, and usually renders it totally unsuitable for cabinet-making, except on those rare occasions when the bending is required for a special purpose.

Shakes are splits in the surface of the wood, and must always be avoided.

large dead knots are a liability and ought to be avoided. They are distinguished by a surrounding black mark. Certain types of tree grow very high before branching out, and these produce long boards which are knot-free.

A badly warped board is not much use to the cabinet-maker. The distortion is caused by uneven drying of the sap in the wood, and tensions arising inside the piece. Another bad fault is known as 'shakes', which are splits or cracks running through a length of timber.

WHERE TO BUY

The Timber Merchant

Arriving at the woodyard, the first thing you notice is that all the timber is stacked high in large, open sheds. Most timber merchants are inevitably limited in the range of woods they stock, especially of the home-grown variety, but you can usually order some of the less well-known species and get them cut to your required sizes.

Although the staff at a timber merchant's are only too willing to help, it is no use relying on them to advise you which wood to select for whatever purpose, or to tell you how much you will need. Whilst they are certain to know their business, they cannot be expected to know yours. So before you enter the woodyard, you should already know what type of wood you are after, and have a complete list of dimensions in your pocket, known as the cutting list, ready to present as your order. You are entitled to inspect the stocks before an order is taken, and to compare prices of similar types of wood.

There should be no problem in obtaining any amount of softwood from the timber merchant. Hardwoods can present more difficulties. The range is often limited, unless the merchant makes a point of keeping a special stock of the lesser-used and more costly woods like English oak, elm, rosewood and such similar examples. However, the African hardwoods like afrormosia, iroko and sapele are not difficult to find.

The Second-Hand Market

This broadly divides into small pricey antique shops and large second-hand furniture warehouses where the prices vary according to the goods. Second-hand dealers trade on the contents of house clearances, and a lot of the stuff that passes through their hands can only be described as useless junk – not that they would admit it! But apart from this, you can often salvage good, well-seasoned hardwood: wardrobes and bed-ends made from solid oak boards. There are other classic hardwoods to be found, like mahogany and rosewood, walnut and teak.

If you know what you want and can recognise the potential value of a broken old cabinet or an unsaleable headboard, you are certain to walk away with a bargain. Take your solid boards to a local joinery, and they will probably agree to plane a fractional amount off the top and bottom faces for a small fee – and that is often when you discover the true value of your wood. The oak or mahogany boards come to life and look as good as new – for a fraction of the cost you would have to pay the timber merchant. But be warned: there is a lot of veneered stuff lying around the second-hand shops.

48

Some of the plywood will come in useful, but the rest is best left where it is.

The second-hand market seems to have a 'think of a number' price list when it comes to discussing business and trying to agree a price on broken furniture. By far the best approach is to pretend that you are doing them a favour by taking the stuff off their hands – in many cases this is the truth anyway. Never be afraid to haggle, and keep a sense of humour at all times. If the idea of spending good money on a broken old table seems perfectly ridiculous, remember that the wood you are getting out of it could have cost you three or four times as much if you had ordered it new from the timber merchant. Also, you have the satisfaction of knowing that the material, if old, is therefore well-seasoned, and that you have not played a part in the felling of the world's rain forests, which is rapidly becoming a serious problem. A final word of caution: watch out for woodworm infestation in all second-hand wood.

A SELECTION OF WOODS

It is not always easy to choose the most appropriate type of wood for the piece you wish to make. Occasionally, the decision is dictated by the nature of the project. For instance, if you set out to build a reproduction-style copy of an oak settle, then you must use oak as your material or forfeit authenticity. But in cases where the choice is less retricted, you can only rely on your own judgement. Below are a few examples from both categories.

Softwoods

Cedar This pale brown wood, relatively light in weight, is obtained from trees which grow to a considerable height before branches appear, providing knot-free boards containing a sweet-smelling aromatic oil which acts as an insect-repellent. Though it is rarely used in the construction of furniture, it serves as a material for lining drawers and fitting out cabinets which reflect the style of the later half of the eighteenth century.

Deal A name given to the redwood variety, including pine. It is mostly obtained from the Baltic region, and may be said to have a straw colour with reddish tinges, which slowly darkens on exposure to light. It is widely used in most aspects of woodwork, has a straight grain and plenty of knots. This last property renders it only suitable for carcase work, unless the knots are to be featured in the finished work.

Parana Pine In some respects, parana pine provides a good compromise between cedar and deal. Grown in South America, it has a smooth, regular texture and few knots, but is more dense than cedar. The colour ranges from light to mid-brown, and there is often a distinctive red tinge. It works well, and has handling qualities similar to hardwoods.

Yew Often associated with a country churchyard, the yew tree yields a very hard and durable wood, reddish-brown in colour. In spite of its close grain and toughness, it possesses an elastic, flexible quality. It is not widely used in furniture-making, but was once a popular material for certain types of chair.

49

Hardwoods

Afrormosia One of the higher quality African woods, afrormosia bears a close resemblance to teak, and is a good substitute for it. Afrormosia has a fine grain, and is a pleasing wood to work with. It is medium brown in colour and, when finished with teak oil, takes on a rich golden shine.

Ash A very pale-coloured wood with a rather coarse grain, it is possible to confuse ash with oak, except that the grain is generally much broader. Ash is an extremely tough wood with a fair amount of springiness and so is used in the framing of curved chairs.

Beech The most distinctive feature of this wood is the regular tiny red flecks set in a straw-coloured or light brown grain. Beech is extensively used in the making of framed furniture, and is ideally suited to steam-bending. It is a hard material, and has a very fine texture.

Elm Tree disease decimated much of the indigenous population, but it is still possible to obtain elm from specialist wood merchants. It is light brown in colour, and was once widely used in the making of chair seats.

Iroko Another of the African hardwoods, iroko shares certain characteristics with afrormosia in that it serves as a useful substitute for teak. It is, however, more coarse than afrormosia, much harder, and has a distinct tendency to blunt the cutting edge of tools. It can vary in colour from a golden brown to dark brown.

Mahogany The finest of the mahoganies are those that are grown in the West Indies and Central America, usually known as Cuban mahogany and Honduras mahogany respectively. There is some variation in colour and texture, but the finest examples are a dark red-brown colour, well-figured, and with a reasonably fine grain. African mahogany is similar, but has a lighter brown content to the colour, which remains overall decidedly red. The strong point of this magnificent wood lies in the refinement of the texture, and the superb finish resulting from stain and polish.

Maple Mainly grown in North America, this light brown, fine-grained wood has good handling properties. Certain types of maple have a highly unusual pattern of marks present throughout the wood, caused by a continual attack from the pecking action of birds during the growth of the tree. The wood is referred to as 'bird's eye maple' because of its distinctive marks.

Oak Undoubtedly the sovereign amongst woods, oak has many classic qualities. English oak has, for many years, been the principal material for all classes of woodwork in the British Isles. It is strong and very durable. Other types of oak come from Eastern Europe, America and Japan; these all have a difference in colour. The grain, however, is easily recognised, and when the log is sawn radially, silver flashes, or streaks, appear on the surface.

Sapele This African wood bears a similarity to mahogany, but the red colour is less pronounced. The grain and texture are very attractive; but the one feature that marks it out from genuine mahogany is that a series of distinctive stripes, or silvery bands, are present in the grain. Another African hardwood in the same family is utile. Between them, sapele and utile serve the cabinet-maker well, providing an excellent substitute for mahogany. They are both hard, easy to work, and produce a fine-quality finish. I would recommend sapele highly for reproduction furniture.

Walnut Much of the furniture built during the 18th century was made from this wood. It is golden brown in colour, fairly hard, close-grained, and has scarcely any tendency to warp or shrink, except in the form of satin walnut. A darker version is American black walnut.

There are, of course, many other woods – some equally well known, others far more obscure – and it is one of the chief pleasures of woodwork to explore new materials. As your knowledge and experience of furniture-making increase, the task of selecting the best wood becomes a matter of instinct.

4 How to Measure and Mark

In all the realms of woodwork there is no aspect more vital to the successful outcome of the workpiece under construction than that of measuring and marking out the material. It precedes every stage, from the moment the first piece of wood is picked up to the time when the final cut is made. In fact, the process begins even earlier, when the item of furniture is planned and a cutting list worked out.

The various tools have already been enumerated; now we shall consider them in greater detail, together with the methods employed when undertaking a typical cabinet-maker's project.

UNITS OF MEASUREMENT

You must first decide which unit of measurement you will use. Two units are available: the inch and the millimetre. At one time all English craftsmen worked in imperial inches, and would have thought of using nothing else, whilst their counterparts on the continent of Europe measured in metric and, therefore, based all their work on the millimetre.

The slow conversion to metric measurement in the British Isles has meant that over the years Britain has become familiar with both systems and, to some extent, accepted that they are interchangeable.

There is, however, nothing more confusing than to start work on a piece of furniture with measurements worked out in feet and inches, converting to millimetres when you order your materials, back to inches for marking out the overall lengths and metric for the joints. This is not to say that it is *impossible* to mix units – there are times when you have no option – but it is generally much more satisfactory to work within one particular system.

As the majority of timber merchants now quote wood sizes in millimetres, you should aim to work entirely in metric. But it is still important to be familiar with imperial measurements, since these are part of the colloquial language of wood.

INITIAL PLANS

Very few people devote their time and energy to cabinet-making merely for the sake of it. Usually they are motivated to make something for their own use, if their interest is purely amateur, or they work professionally to supply the demand for high-quality hand-made furniture.

The first step is to make a plan. Whoever is to receive the end product, whether it is yourself or a customer, you need to decide exactly what sort of piece you are going to build, how big it will be, what purpose it is to serve and which type of wood you intend using in its construction.

If it is your intention to design your project in a reproduction style, you have a wealth of furniture to imitate. Although it is always advisable to aim for historical accuracy, you have complete control over the choice of period, and the judicious mixing of styles can often produce something that is at once practical, sensitive and endowed with a beauty for which you can claim full responsibility.

Ideas often come from pieces of furniture that you see on display in such diverse places as other people's houses, stately homes, furnishing stores, books and magazines. Your initial plan may be no more than a simple sketch, adapting what you have seen to suit your own taste and purpose. It must inevitably take account of scale, and you should quickly be able to transform your early ideas into a proper drawing, showing the plan and elevations. This might sound an extremely elaborate way of setting about the task, but how else can you determine whether the proportions are to your liking?

This is also the time to decide what materials you will employ. Traditional furniture almost always calls for the use of hardwood – though there are some exceptions – and the fittings, such as hinges, door handles and locks must also be decided upon.

Finally, your plan must show the overall dimensions, in order for the next stage to proceed satisfactorily.

THE CUTTING LIST

Before you visit your timber supplier, the plan of your workpiece must be broken down into its component parts. Each item of material is noted according to its length, width and thickness, and similar pieces are arranged in groups. The result is what is known as a cutting list.

When you compile your cutting list, several points need to be considered. The first of these is the question of economy. Good-quality timber is never cheap, and nobody wants to spend more than they have to. As already stated, when buying planed wood you are advised to choose cross-sections which can be obtained from sawn wood of the nearest possible size, thus avoiding the purchase of excessive amounts.

There is, however, one good reason for ordering too much – and that is in the lengths of the individual pieces. It is customary to allow a small amount of waste at each end of the wood when certain joints are being cut, so that you are left with at least some margin of safety against the chance of the wood splitting. The excess is then trimmed before assembly begins.

A third point is worth bearing in mind: ordering short lengths and pieces which generally fail to conform to convenient round figures. When several short pieces of the same cross-section are required, the usual procedure is to add up their total length, take this amount to the nearest metre or foot in an upward direction and quote this in the order. When the design calls for curved pieces to be included, these are normally marked from templates, so clearly the wood from which they are cut must be large enough to receive the templates and still allow a little extra as waste.

Once you have compiled the full cutting list, present this to your timber merchant, specifying the type of wood you want and stating plainly whether the sizes are 'finished' or 'sawn'.

On the occasions when you acquire your wood from second-hand sources, such as the breaking up of old scrap furniture, the cutting list does not need to be quite so precise, since you will probably be sawing and planing your own lengths.

USING THE TAPE-MEASURE

We all adopt our own favourite methods of measuring wood. The retractable steel tape-measure is recommended because it is so compact and easy to use. A small lip

When the retractable steel tape-measure is used to measure the wood, the special lip at the end of the tape is hooked over the edge of the wood to provide a zero position. For greatest accuracy, it is advisable to measure from the first inch position, or 100mm in the case of the metric scale, and then subtract this amount from the overall measurement.

serves to hook over the edge of the material to be measured, automatically providing a zero position. Imperial and metric graduations are clearly printed on the upper surface of the tape, allowing you to make quick comparisons or accurate conversions.

Always take care when reading the increments on the scale. The tape measure, like the two-foot rule, is a precision instrument. There is an old saying exhorting you to 'measure twice and cut once', and this is wise advice which even the most experienced woodworker should heed.

Once you have found the required position along the scale, make a small mark against it in pencil. Do not press too hard with the point of the pencil or you will dent the surface of the wood.

SQUARING OFF THE WOOD

In most marking operations, a straight line must be drawn perpendicularly across the grain of the wood, usually as a preparatory step for sawing or cutting out joints. For right-angled lines the square is placed with its wooden handle bearing against the edge of the wood, so that the pencil point can be drawn in the desired position along the steel blade.

When the wood must be squared around on all four surfaces, as for marking the shoulders of a tenon, there is a standard procedure which ensures that the lines meet perfectly. The method involves holding the square against two adjacent faces of the wood, known as 'face side' and 'face edge'. For purposes of identification, face side refers to the width of the wood, and face edge to the

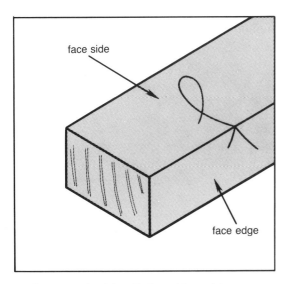

Markings used to identify face side and face edge.

thickness. Obviously, only one width and one thickness apply. By convention, the former is marked in pencil with an elongated loop and the latter with a short 'V'. If all four plane positions are set from these two faces, accuracy is assured.

For marking out mitre joints and other purposes calling for 45 degree angles, the mitre square is used in conjunction with the square. An adjustable multi-purpose mitre square can be employed to fulfil both functions. The technique of working the square from face side and face edge also applies in this case.

Several narrow pieces of wood may be squared off at the same time if they are of equal length, provided the blade of the square reaches across their combined

The four positions of the square for marking all around the wood from face side and face edge (*see* above and overleaf).

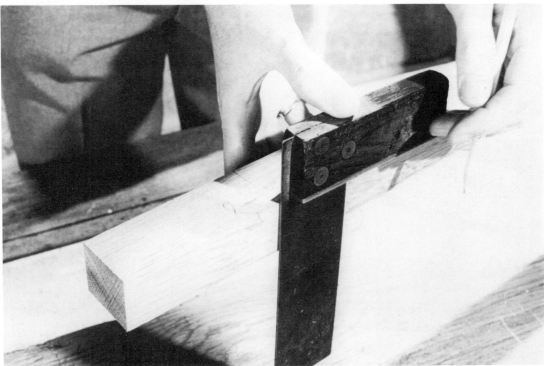

width. Before adopting this method, check that all the individual lengths butt exactly up against each other. It only takes one slightly bent piece to throw out the marked line and lead to an error which could later prove to be very costly.

USING THE MARKING GAUGE

The marking gauge has an important role to play in preparing the wood for cutting and jointing. Its single spur is used to score a thin line along the surface of the wood parallel to the edge.

The position of the spur is set by slackening off the screw that holds the fence firmly against the stock, and sliding the fence until the distance that separates it from the spur is equal to the required setting. This distance is either measured by placing the end of the tape-measure against the face of the fence and moving it back and forth until the reading on the tape coincides with the spur, or the measurement can be made directly on the surface of the wood, and the marking gauge adjusted so that when the fence bears against the edge of the wood, the spur just touches the pencil mark. Tighten the screw to hold the fence securely in place on the stock.

The gauge is manipulated by pressing the fence against the wood and, with the point of the spur just touching the surface, running it for the required distance. Pressure must be maintained for the full duration of the marking, because the spur can easily fall into a groove in the grain and wander off line as the grain slightly changes direction. It is a good idea to make two or three strokes of the gauge, exerting only mild downward pressure with the first run to cut a path and deepening the incision with each subsequent stroke.

USING THE MORTISE GAUGE

The main difference between the mortise gauge and the marking gauge is in the number of spurs; the marking gauge has one, as described, whereas the mortise gauge has two, one of which may be adjusted.

Firstly, the gap between the two spurs is altered by turning the thumbscrew at the far end of the stem, or by pushing back and forth on the slider, until the distance between the points is equal to the width of a chisel nearest to the size of the mortise that you intend cutting. Secondly, the fence of the gauge is adjusted, in the same manner as for the marking gauge, until the two parallel lines inscribed by the spurs coincide with the required position.

The mortise lines are usually set at the centre of the wood, and a certain amount of fine adjustment will be necessary with the fence. You can easily tell when the lines are properly centralised, by holding the gauge against each of the two edges and pressing the two points down into the surface. The impressions will be the same from either direction.

The most effective way of holding the gauge is to grasp it with the fence coming between thumb and forefinger and the remaining three fingers tucked around the stem.

The mortise gauge is held firmly between finger and thumb, with the remaining fingers grasped around the stock. The correct procedure is to place the fence against the face side or face edge of the wood being marked.

TEMPLATES

A template is understood to mean any piece of material which is cut to form a pattern; in the case of woodwork, it is normally made from thin plywood or thick cardboard.

Templates are used for a variety of reasons. The two most common applications are when a complicated shape demands precise preparation with special drawing implements on a piece of material which can easily be cut with a sharp knife, so that the shape can be appraised

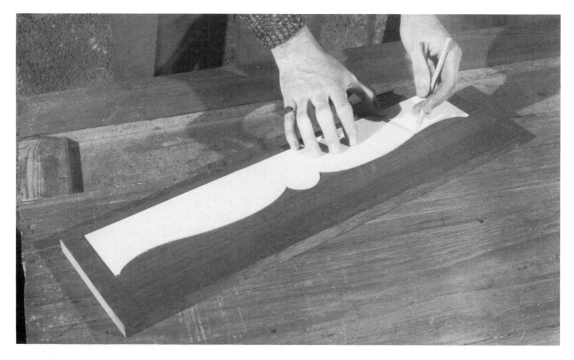

Templates are used when the wood requires a particular curve or pattern which must be drawn with great precision and often repeated on several pieces of wood. Templates may be cut from thick card or thin plywood.

before embarking on the cutting of the wood; and for making a pattern which needs to be duplicated with great accuracy several times, such as the preparation of a curved leg.

Unless many copies are needed, cardboard is a better material than plywood for templates because it is easy to cut and trim. Also, it may be pinned on to a drawing board for the marking out process, using T-square, set squares and a pair of geometrical compasses.

When the template has been successfully cut out and approved, it is laid carefully on the wood, making sure that it is correctly positioned with respect to the direction of the grain, and marked around in pencil.

MARKING SCREW POSITIONS

Screws have many uses in cabinet-making, either as part of the general assembling of the workpiece or to attach the various fittings that often make up part of the finished article. Whatever their purpose, the screws all share one common need – and that is for their positions to be clearly and effectively marked on the surface of the wood.

When the screw forms a part of the cabinet assembly, it is located by measuring with the tape measure and marking in pencil. In the case of mounting a hinge or handle, the fitting itself provides an accurate guide to the positioning of the screw holes and, once again, a small pencil mark should be made to indicate the correct place.

Before attempting to drill holes in the wood, all screw positions must be further marked with the bradawl, in which the pointed tip is pressed down into the wood, making a deep impression that acts as a pilot hole for the drill bit. Indeed, on occasions when you need to fit small brass screws, such as those used to mount a typical cabinet door lock, the bradawl actually serves the purpose of making the hole, since any short screw, when driven in with a screwdriver, will cut its own path and needs no further drilling.

IDENTIFYING MARKED OUT WOOD

As a period of time may elapse before each piece of marked wood is cut or sawn on the work-bench, it is only sensible to devise some form of identification so that you know exactly which length relates to each part of the plan. You will also want to distinguish the unwanted waste portions from the main parts of the wood.

Numbering or lettering several identical lengths of wood will keep them separate and quickly identify where they are intended to fit. All coded markings should be written lightly on the surface in soft pencil or wax crayon, both of which can easily be removed after assembly by rubbing down with sandpaper.

For all waste portions, make a series of criss-cross pencil lines to show where joints must be cut and excess lengths trimmed back.

5 How to Cut and Shape

After the wood has been carefully measured out and marked, it is ready to be cut to size. Various techniques have been devised to help you obtain the best results in cutting and shaping the wood, and I will now examine these in detail.

SAWING TECHNIQUES

Preliminary Sawing

It has already been stated that the handsaw is used in the initial stage of cutting the wood, but this must not be taken to mean that the tool can be wielded in any way. Even a preliminary cut should be executed as accurately as possible. It usually entails cutting various pieces of prepared wood to length, and may well be required before the main marking out can begin.

Never guess where to cut the wood. If a large piece needs to be divided up into several shorter lengths, mark each section clearly by squaring all around in pencil. This presents you with four straight lines which all meet up at the four corners of the wood, and one slight problem – each pencil line will be much thinner than the width of the saw kerf. If the individual lengths need to be exact, you will have to allow for the kerf by always sawing just on the waste side of the line, and obviously this waste must not be permitted to encroach on the length of the next piece. A second squared line must therefore be marked nearby, thus placing the saw cuts in a sort of no man's land.

Before starting to saw, it is wise to hold the wood steady so that it cannot move, rather than attempting to grasp it free hand on the top of the work-bench to find that it moves around and spoils the direction of the saw cut. There are several ways of securing the wood: it can be placed in the vice; clamped to the side of the work-bench so that the marked line overhangs the end; or it can be held by hand in the bench hook, which helps to hold it firm. I work on the principle of placing large, heavy sections of wood in the vice, often supported at the far end; clamping medium-sized pieces to the workbench; and holding small lengths in the bench hook.

Take the saw in your cutting hand, gripping it with your forefinger pointing forwards in the direction of the saw blade, and carefully place it on the squared pencil line, resting it so that the teeth are just to the waste side of the line. With your other hand, hold the wood in such a way that by bending your thumb you bear against the side of the saw blade with your knuckle joint.

Draw the saw backwards to make the first cut, observing closely to make sure that the kerf is formed against the line. When you can see that all is well, work the saw gently back and forth to increase the cut further along the pencil line. It is important that the blade is kept absolutely vertical. Once the first few strokes have been made, and the kerf established, you can increase the speed of the cut and exert more force.

As you reach a point approximately half-way through the wood, it is advisable to stop, take the piece and turn it over to start again from the opposite side so that the saw cuts meet in the middle. This prevents splits from occurring on the bottom, as would happen if the saw were allowed to pass straight through. For a large section of wood, call on the assistance of a second person to hold the free end of the wood so that it does not drop off suddenly and damage itself falling to the ground.

Joint Sawing

The main difference between preliminary sawing and the cutting out of a joint is in the degree of absolute precision. After all, even in the earlier stage of cutting the wood to length, it was necessary to follow a marked line and keep to the waste side of it. The only difference was that the saw, in the form of the relatively large handsaw, has teeth designed for quick cutting and a long blade which has a tendency to flex.

For joint sawing, turn instead to the tenon saw, which has a strengthened back to prevent the blade from bending, and smaller teeth of increased frequency to make for a more exact and refined cut.

The handsaw or tenon saw is held by taking a firm grip on the handle, and pointing the forefinger forward in the direction of the saw blade.

In this case, the tenon saw is employed after the wood has been marked with pencil lines and with inscribed markings from the mortise or marking gauge. Whether it is cut into the end-grain to produce a tenon or sawn across the grain to produce a halved joint, a bridle joint or a dovetail joint, the principle is the same – there is no room for error.

The cutting of a tenon does not present a problem, at least not in the first stage of preparation. The marked out piece is placed at an angle of 45 degrees in the vice, and the saw cut made on the waste side of the two gauged lines running on the two edges and the end-grain. Because the saw is being worked in the same direction as the grain, it easily makes its initial cut and proceeds onwards with accuracy.

When you come to cut away the shoulders by laying the wood flat on the workbench or bench hook it is a different story, because the tenon saw is being asked to cut at right-angles to the grain. It is true that this is what the tool is primarily designed for, but there is the inherent problem that when the saw is worked across the grain, it often has a habit of drifting slightly one way or the other, scuffing the surface with its teeth. We must find a way of ensuring that the cut follows the marked shoulder line and nothing else.

This is achieved by placing the square back in position so that it lines up exactly with the pencil mark denoting the shoulder of the tenon, and scoring along the line with a sharp knife. Remove the square, take hold of a chisel and pare away a sloped channel on the waste side of the line to create a groove in which the tenon saw can be placed. The saw cut can now be made with accuracy, knowing

Before making a saw cut across the grain of the wood, it is good practice to cut a shallow angled channel with the chisel on the waste side of the marked line, in which the saw blade can run.

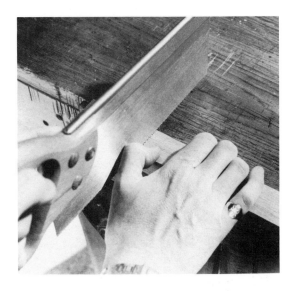

When commencing a cut with the tenon saw, line up the saw blade and position the knuckle of your thumb against it to act as a guide. Once the first few strokes of the saw have started off the cut, you can remove your thumb and continue sawing with a quicker, firmer action.

that the first few strokes will be guided by the channel. This method is rigorously applied to all shoulder lines, for tenons, halved joints, bridle joints, housing joints and dovetail joints.

Coping Saw

This tool, consisting of a deep frame with a detachable blade, is used to cut curves. Always clamp the wood securely in the vice so that you can guide the blade with great accuracy. Outside curves present little problem, provided they do not plunge so deeply into the wood that there is not sufficient room for the frame to operate without binding.

The coping saw is particularly useful in its ability to cut holes inside the wood.

You start by drilling out a hole near to the marked line, just on the waste side, then unscrew the handle of the saw so that the blade may be detached. Pass its free end through the drilled hole, re-attach it to the frame and tighten up the handle. From now on, the blade can be made to work entirely within the hole, cutting around the perimeter until the waste drops out.

Jigsaw

The jigsaw can be used in place of the handsaw for the first stage of cutting out the wood, and the coping saw for cutting curves. It cannot take over from the tenon saw for the accurate cutting of joints, except in rare circumstances.

For cutting out holes inside the wood, use the coping saw.

Because it works at high speed, the jigsaw has the potential to cut very rapidly, creating a lot of fine sawdust. The blades are normally quite flexible and you must beware its habit of failing to cut a perfectly square edge, especially in some of the denser hardwoods which offer more resistance. With experience, you can easily judge the correct rate of progress for a particular species of wood. Remember to check the blade for sharpness, and replace it at the first sign of wear.

CHISELLING TECHNIQUES

Chopping Out

The main purpose of the chisel is to provide the woodworker with a fast and efficient way of chopping out mortises, housing joints, halved joints and dovetail joints. In the case of the mortise, a great deal of the waste is first removed with a drill, but the shaping of the square or rectangular hole still depends on the chisel.

The chopping action is carried out in two stages. For the first stage, where the chisel is worked quickly to remove a lot of waste, it is held at an angle with the flat face of the blade pointing towards the centre of the mortise and the tool gradually worked back towards both ends. As you progress from the centre, so the angle should change from an initial 45 degrees until the blade is almost vertical. At this point, as you approach the end of the mortise, turn the chisel around so that the flat face is towards the end, and make a final downward cut on the marked line.

The blade must always be kept razor-

The correct way to hold the chisel for chopping.

sharp, or you will find that the chopping action results in a clumsy hacking of the grain instead of clean cuts revealing smooth end-grain.

Paring

The second use of the chisel is to pare away thin slices of wood from the surface, rather as if you were manually planing it. It is a technique which is employed to cut back the cheeks of a tenon, the two joining surfaces of a halved joint or the sides of the pins and sockets of a dovetail joint, so that small amounts of wood may be removed in the process of fitting a joint together. A similar paring action can be used for preparing chamfers and bevels.

The correct way to hold the chisel for paring.

PLANING TECHNIQUES

Planing along the Grain

After the wood has been marked out in pencil and cut with the saw, it is usual to plane the edges flat. For one thing, no matter how carefully you saw, it is very difficult to acheive a line that is truly straight, and in working it on the waste side of the line, there is nearly always a little of the waste still to be removed.

You might think that there is nothing easier than planing in the same direction as the grain and, indeed, you would be correct. The thought conjures up a mental picture of the smoothing plane progressing crisply along the edge, a thin, continuous shaving curling up from the blade. But wait – before you mount the wood in the vice and start planing, remember that there are two possible directions in which you can plane along the same direction as the grain. And unless the wood is absolutely straight-grained, these two directions will not produce equal results. Try working the blade from one end and the result is a perfect shaving and a flat smooth edge; but work it from the opposite end and the edge scuffs up into ridges and bits of loose fibre. Why should this be so?

If you examine the side of the piece and look carefully for the grain, you will often see that it runs at a slight angle to the edges. Sometimes it forms a wavy, undulating pattern, running upwards in one direction for part of the wood's length before dipping down again. But, in general, there is some consistency to the way it is inclined.

The trick is to avoid working the plane against the angle, in other words, in such a way that if you viewed the wood from behind the plane, you would see the grain coming up towards you. Instead, it should be rising upward in the same direction as that in which the plane is travelling.

Planing across the Grain

In contrast to the previous method, there is no need to worry about which direction you choose when planing across the grain – in other words, planing along the end-grain – because either way around you are working the blade more or less at right-angles to the grain's direction.

The problem in planing across the grain is encountered at the end of each stroke, for the blade frequently splits away the last fraction of an inch, thus creating a problem when it comes to planing along the grain, since you are forced to reduce the width of the wood in order to achieve a clean, straight edge.

So something must clearly be done to

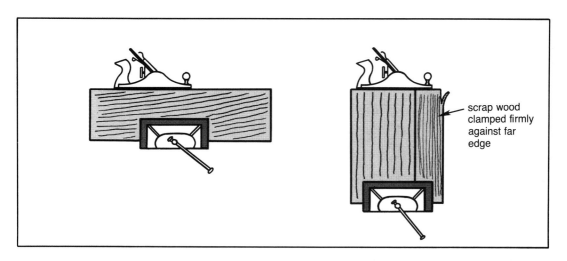

scrap wood clamped firmly against far edge

Two rules apply to the planing of wood along the grain and across the end grain. In the first case (left), you should arrange for the smoothing plane to travel in the same direction as the upward inclination of the grain, rather than against it. In the second case (right), a block of scrap wood is clamped against the far edge of the workpiece, so that the end grain forms a continuous surface and thus ensures that any splitting of the wood occurs on the waste.

prevent the end from splitting. The usual way is to clamp a second piece of wood which measures exactly the same thickness to the far edge so that its end-grain is flush with that of the workpiece. As the plane progresses along the end-grain it reaches the end of the workpiece but runs immediately on to the scrap piece, so this receives the split edge.

Alternatively, measure the workpiece wider than you need, and plane along the end-grain first, so that if the wood splits at the end of the cut, at least you know that the width will have to be trimmed anyway.

DRILLING TECHNIQUES

Stopped Drilling

Whatever type of drill bit you use, it is important to know how deeply you are boring into the wood and thus prevent the hole from sinking too far down. The depth can be controlled by the simple expedient of fitting a guide to the shaft of the bit. This may take the form either of a plastic collar which is supplied with certain types of bit, or a piece of self-adhesive tape can be stuck on to indicate the required depth.

Through Drilling

The problem that arises when you drill right through a piece of wood is that the drill bit splinters the underside as it breaks through, causing damage to the surrounding surface. This is avoided in two ways. Firstly, you can clamp the workpiece tightly on top of a length of smooth-surfaced scrap wood so that the two sides come into contact. As the drill bit reaches the point at which it emerges from the underside of the first piece, it

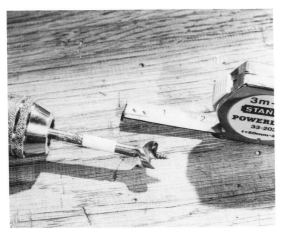

A simple depth guide can be made for the drill bit by binding a length of sticky tape around the stem at the required distance.

passes directly into the top face of the scrap piece as if the two were joined together. When the scrap piece is removed, you will find a perfect edge to the hole in the workpiece.

The alternative method is to drill the hole with a centre bit or auger which has a pointed tip. Drill down into the wood until the tip just begins to break through on the underside, then take it out, turn the wood over and place the point of the bit in the tiny hole. Commence drilling again, until the two parts of the same hole meet somewhere in the middle.

6 Fixing Wood Together

Whenever two or more pieces of wood need to be joined together, the resulting union must be made permanently secure. The wood may be fixed by one of several means, the choice usually depending on the nature of the joint and the use to which it will be put.

There are four basic methods available to the cabinet-maker. The first is a surface bond created by applying glue or adhesive to the two joining surfaces. The second method is to hold the wood together by driving through it either a screw, nail or a wooden peg, or some variation of the same idea. This is immediately effective, and requires no time-lapse, as glue does. Thirdly, a joint can be made by introducing an intermediate fixture, such as a joining block or a solid bracket. The fourth method is to make a moveable joint, using hinges and pivots, to open and close cupboard doors or fold up table legs.

In practice, each of these four methods often relies upon one of the other three, and sometimes perhaps all of them. Hence the commonly used instruction telling you to assemble 'with glue and screws'. The glue holds the abutting surfaces together, and the screws add an important reinforcement.

GLUES AND ADHESIVES

Strictly speaking, a glue is derived from animal or vegetable matter and is therefore an organic substance. Adhesive is synthetic in origin, being composed chiefly of chemicals mixed into either a dry powder to which water must be added before use, or a liquid solution which is often highly volatile due to the presence of solvents in the mixture.

Traditional craftsmen still work with glue, but most woodworkers rely on adhesives. Since the main object of this book is to describe the fundamental techniques which relate to the making of household furniture, using methods which have been employed for many years, the term 'glue' shall be taken to mean any substance which has the ability to join two parts of an assembly, no matter how it has been made.

Scotch or Animal Glue

This strong-smelling glue is probably the most complicated to prepare. It is supplied as a solid cake which firstly has to be wrapped in a piece of cloth and struck with a hammer to break it up into small fragments. These are then placed in a special glue-pot, covered with cold water and left for up to a day to soak thoroughly. The glue-pot is then heated at the work-bench on a burner until the solids are completely dissolved to form a thick syrup, then brought to the boil and left simmering. The glue must not be boiled for a long time, or it will darken in colour and lose much of its strength.

Before being applied to the joint, it is

usual to warm the surfaces of the wood. The glue is worked into the joint with a brush, and as the process of cooling begins, it gradually returns to the solid state and makes for a strong bond. However, animal glue is neither heat- nor water-resistant, and is prone to fungal attack, so it clearly has its limitations.

The modern range of synthetic glues have mostly replaced Scotch glue, leaving it largely for furniture restoration and the perfectionist cabinet-maker producing high-class reproduction pieces. It is not recommended for the amateur woodworker and furniture-maker.

Powdered Resin Glue

Although there seems to be an apparently endless list of synthetic substances on the market, our interest is chiefly concentrated on the urea formaldehyde powdered resin type, to which a measured quantity of cold water must be added and stirred in thoroughly, making for an active and workable mixture which is ready for use within a matter of minutes.

You can probably get your hands on an old cup, and this will serve as a suitable mixing vessel. To apply the glue, use a small, cheap artist's paintbrush. Temperature does not play a critical role in the use of this glue, except to say that an ambient temperature of at least 41°F(15°C) is desirable. When you have finished with the glue, rinse out the cup and the brush in warm water, to which a few drops of washing-up liquid have been added. This mild soap solution will get rid of all the glue down to the last trace, after which the cup and brush should be washed thoroughly in cold water.

To mix a quantity of powdered resin wood glue, you need a clean vessel like an old cup, a measuring spoon, stirrer, and a brush to apply the glue mixture to the work.

Ready-Mixed Liquid Glue

This is another synthetic glue which does not need any preparation whatsoever, but can be applied directly to the work-piece, straight from the tube or bottle. By chemical composition it is known as polyvinyl acetate (PVA).

Choosing a Glue

The strength of a good glue lies in its ability to spread in liquid form across the full extent of the joining surfaces and cover a relatively big area. If you could examine the surface of the wood in microscopic detail, you would discover that no matter how smooth it appears to the naked eye or feels to the touch, it is, in fact, totally irregular and full of tiny cavities. The glue, possessing the capacity to flow, searches out these holes or crevices, and fills them. As it begins to set, so the internal molecular structure of the glue locks into a chain and eventually becomes a single solid mass, often stronger than the wood itself.

The conditions necessary for a successful bond are that the two joining surfaces be clean, dry and free from traces of oil or grease. Once the glue has been applied to both parts of the joint, it is assembled and clamped firmly together for a period of time whilst the glue sets hard.

You cannot be involved in woodwork and cabinet-making without developing a preference for one type of glue. For the vast majority of furniture construction, Cascamite is my favourite, as it gives a strong, durable and waterproof bond. Its only real drawback is that it will not take a wood stain, and therefore all traces of it must be removed from the surface of the wood including any visible gaps in the joints. This is best carried out before the glue has had a chance to dry by taking a soft moistened cloth and wiping around the joints where any of the glue has seeped out. If any small blobs pass undetected, they can normally be scraped off very carefully with the blade of a chisel, and the area rubbed down with a fine-grade sandpaper. Small cracks between joints can then be filled with wood stopper.

SCREWS, NAILS AND PEGS

Before examining these three items in detail, you must remember the important fact that we are dealing with the techniques associated with the creation of good-quality furniture. We have become so accustomed to seeing self-assembly furniture made from composite materials such as veneered chipboard passing itself off as an acceptable imitation of the real thing, that the newcomer to the subject could easily be misled into believing that such materials automatically have a place on the craftsman's work-bench. They have not, and nor have the profusion of fixings and accessories like double-threaded cross-head screws and plastic dowels.

Screws

Most standard cabinet work demands the use of the countersunk mild steel or brass woodscrew with a single slot cut in the head.

Before a screw can be fitted, a hole needs to be bored in the wood to receive it. Softwoods and hardwoods both share basically the same composition. They are made up from tightly-packed strands of fibrous material to form the main substance of the wood. The arrangement in both size and direction of the particles and fibres within the wood is the grain.

The spiral thread of the screw is designed to clasp hold of these fibres and grip them tenaciously, but the screw can only have its maximum holding effect if it is fitted at right-angles to the direction of the grain. Once that angle decreases, so the thread has less ability to wrap itself around the fibrous strands of the wood, until eventually, when it lies in the same direction as the grain, it has no holding ability whatsoever. It follows, then, that a screw should always be driven perpendicular to the grain, and never into end-grain. If you attempt the latter, you will discover that the screw acts rather like a drill bit and makes a hole from which it can be extracted quite easily.

When you need to drive a screw into end-grain, you must firstly drill out a hole near to the end of the wood, but at right-angles to the grain, and glue a piece of dowelling into the hole. This provides the means of effectively screwing across the grain of the dowel material, giving the desired grip. Plywood has similar properties to softwood and hardwood, except that each layer of ply rests at 90 degrees to its neighbour, so that all the edges present a certain amount of grain, as well as end-grain.

The hole for a countersunk woodscrew is bored into the wood with a drill bit that matches the size of the screw – for example, a number 6 or number 8 gauge – and the end of the bit tapers to a point just like the profile of the screw.

Certain woods, such as oak, contain an acid which reacts with mild steel to leave a blue stain around the head of the

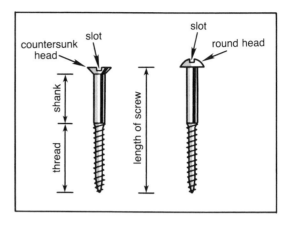

The two most common types of screw used in cabinet work.

Fitting a dowel through the wood permits screwing into the end-grain. Once secured in place with glue, the dowel effectively offers some cross-grain for the thread of the screw to take hold.

screw; it is therefore customary to fit brass screws instead, unless the screw holes are well out of sight. Brass is a much softer material than steel. It is an alloy of copper and zinc, and it has a nasty habit of shearing under heavy load. So when using brass screws, it is wise to employ a larger size screw than might appear necessary. Alternatively, drill out the hole in the wood and fit a mild steel screw first, so that it cuts the thread and bears the brunt of the initial load. Take out the steel screw, and fit an identical-sized brass screw in its place.

When fitting very small screws, make a hole in the wood using the point of the bradawl. Tap the screw partly into the hole with a tack hammer, and screw it in the rest of the way with a small cabinet screwdriver, taking care to keep it perpendicular to the surface of the wood.

Nails

Nails are very widely used in general carpentry and joinery, but in the field of cabinet-making their application is extremely limited. Unlike the woodscrew, a nail's long, slender shape makes it ideal for driving into end-grain, where it takes a firmer hold than if it had been driven across the grain. However, such instances should rarely arise in the making of good-quality furniture.

It is true that when you dismantle certain items of old furniture, you will occasionally find that nails have been used to hold a mortise and tenon joint in place, often supplementing the brittle Scotch glue which was once so widely employed. This was not good practice, and is to be deplored. By the same token, nails have also been used to attach table-tops to their frames and stool seats to

their legs, but these are equally bad habits and must not be taken as acceptable fixing methods.

There should be no need to use nails at all in the assembling of the main joints. For most joints, glue alone is sufficient; but when it does require some form of reinforcement, the usual procedure is to fit screws, pegs, or wooden wedges, depending on the type of joint and where it is placed with respect to the workpiece.

Nails are most useful for fitting items of trim, edge mouldings, intricate wooden carvings and any other sort of surface decoration. Even so, glue should still be applied to the joining surfaces. The nails most suited to the purpose are panel pins and veneer pins; they are very thin and bend easily, and must be tapped carefully into the wood with a tack hammer. When the small heads are flush with the surface of the wood, punch them in further with the blunted end of a large wire nail, and fill the hole with wood stopper.

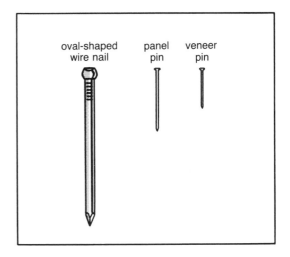

The most common types of nail and pin used in cabinet work.

Pegs

The wooden peg is an extension, or perhaps more accurately a predecessor, of the nail and the screw. It has a place in the assembling of mortise and tenon joints where the sections of wood are rather large and subject to stresses and heavy loads. When oak was widely used in the making of general items of joinery, it was customary to peg the joints together. A special technique is applied to the pegged mortise and tenon joint, known as 'draw-boring', in which holes are drilled through the two parts of the joint, the one in the tenon slightly offset from that in the mortise, so that as the peg is driven in, it pulls the two parts tightly together.

But the peg has an additional and more diverse application than simply pinning joints into place. It can be used in its own right to make the dowel joint, in which two pieces of wood are firstly butted side-by-side, or end-grain to side, and then joined by having a series of wooden dowels glued into holes drilled in corresponding positions in the two abutting faces.

JOINING BLOCKS

Wooden blocks will be found in a lot of old furniture, helping to join a panel to a frame, or reinforcing the corner joints of a chair. They are often cut in a triangular shape. A true craftsman will always strive to make his own blocks from a matching wood to that used for the main sections of the workpiece, knowing that there are always plenty of off-cuts ready to hand.

Blocks used to assemble the panels of a cabinet to its frame tend to be long and narrow, and are fixed in position with glue, whilst clamps hold them securely in place as the glue sets. Corner blocks

Wooden joining blocks.

for chair legs and the supporting framework for cabinets are invariably shaped like equilateral triangles, with a square portion cut from the apex to fit around the leg or post, and they are normally assembled with glue and screws.

BRACKETS

Solid metal brackets have many uses, from supporting cabinet shelves to strengthening corner joints. They rely on screws to attach them to the wood. A variation on the same theme is the flat metal plate designed to join a wooden table top to its frame. The idea is that one of the fixing holes is deliberately elongated to give room for the wood to expand or contract with the changing humidity of the atmosphere, thus preventing a more rigid type of attachment from setting up stresses and strains that would inevitably lead to the wood splitting. Such an arrangement is frequently found on larger tables where scope for movement within the wood is comparatively great – though it is just as valid to consider the same method for attaching a stool seat to its legs.

HINGES

These are supplied in a wide range of sizes and designs, enabling any type of door to be fitted to any sort of cabinet. Hinges are made in various metals, the most suitable of which is undoubtedly brass; some are plain while others are very ornate. All have one thing in common – they are attached to the woodwork with screws. Hinges are rarely glued, and they should never be nailed. Butt hinges and backflap hinges are recessed into the wood, but intricately-patterned hinges are made to fit on the surface of the woodwork.

PIVOTS

There are certain pieces of furniture, namely gate-legged tables, in which a pair of gates swing outwards from the main leg framework to support two hinged table flaps. These rely on the action of a pivot for the smooth opening and closing of the moving parts. It is common practice for the pivot to be made from hardwood dowelling, but a more durable material would be a length of steel rod.

Another type of pivot, such as that installed on either side of a tilting cheval or dressing-table mirror to attach the mirror to its frame, is provided by a screw-thread fitted with a handle or knob so that there is a tightening facility which allows the mirror to be swung into any position within its frame and held firm.

Pivots are not purchased as distinct fittings, but are specially made up from a number of selected materials to serve a particular purpose. Screws and nails each have a part to play, and with a little imagination the skilled cabinet-maker can adapt most of the forementioned fixing methods to good advantage and solve virtually any problem.

7 Wood Finishes

When you have devoted so much time to the making of a piece of furniture, it is only natural that you should want to give it the finest quality finish. Choosing the right type of finish for a particular item is equally as important as cutting the joints properly – in fact it is probably of greater importance, since it is on the appearance of the outer surfaces that the success of the piece is usually judged.

Various wood finishes are available, and they each have their own special handling properties and characteristics. For example, the type of finish that would be suitable for a wall cabinet made from a close-grained hardwood is unlikely to be right for a coarser grained hardwood table, a softwood cabinet or an outdoor seat. Each finish must be selected according to the wood that has been used, whether it is intended for interior or exterior furniture, the amount of use to which the piece will be put during its lifetime, and the degree of refinement that you wish to obtain.

PREPARING THE WOOD

Most preparatory work is concerned with ensuring that the surface of the wood is smooth and free from the tiny imperfections that can so easily become apparent after the finish has been applied. We already know that wood is made up from many fibrous strands, tightly packed together. When it is sawn into boards these fibres are extremely prominent and give the surface a rough feel. Some types of wood have soft fibres, whilst others are harsh to the touch and easily yield splinters.

After the wood has been planed, much of this original coarseness is transformed into clean, smooth sides and edges, although there is often some lifting of the grain, which gives a somewhat irregular feel. You will find that if you run your fingers in one direction along the grain, the wood has a distinctly rough feel rather like a fine stubble, but in the opposite direction it is perfectly smooth. The object is to achieve perfection, however the surface is touched.

In addition, the wood is marked up with a variety of pencil lines during the building of the workpiece, either to indicate where the joints are to be cut, or to identify one piece from another, and these must all be removed from the outer surfaces. It is not quite so important to give the same attention to those surfaces that will remain out of sight, although it must be said that the sign of a good cabinet-maker is the amount of care devoted to all aspects of the work, whether they can be seen or not.

Sandpaper

The means most commonly used to prepare the surfaces of the wood is to rub them down with sandpaper. There are various grades of paper available, rang-

Sandpaper should be wrapped around a block of wood to give a flat, perfectly even surface, and worked back and forth in long, sweeping strokes.

ing from very coarse to very fine. The furniture-maker will find that there are few occasions when the need arises for the coarser grades, as these score the surface of the wood and invariably damage the grain. For the first stage of rubbing down, use a medium-grade sandpaper which will get rid of all pencil marks and take off most of the residual coarseness. Follow this with the finest of papers to leave the silkiest of finishes.

Mention has already been made in the chapter on woods about how it is possible to salvage much excellent hardwood material from old, unwanted furniture. Apart from the financial savings, this is a particularly satisfactory way of obtaining wood because it often enables you to lay your hands on certain types which have become scarce and, consequently, very expensive, and there is the added knowledge and satisfaction that you are in-

dulging in the craft without placing a demand on the world's vanishing forests.

Most of this second-hand wood must be put through a planing machine to skim off a thin amount from both sides to reveal fresh wood beneath; however, sometimes this is not considered desirable, either because the boards you wish to use are too wide to pass through the planer, or because their original thickness is exactly what you want. Provided the surfaces have not been badly scratched or gouged, there is no reason why you should not remove all the old polish or varnish and cut all the sections you need straight from the boards.

Stripping off Old Finishes

There are several ways of completely stripping off old paint or varnish. In most areas there will be a commercial wood-stripping service available which uses a caustic soda bath to remove all traces of the covering. The cost of this service is normally very reasonable and will undoubtedly save you much time and trouble.

You can, of course, do the work yourself using a proprietary paste or chemical stripper. Avoid using the type which can discolour the surface of the wood with its chemical action.

Some removers will rid the wood of the toughest paint and polyurethane-type varnishes without damaging or discolouring the grain. A quantity of the chemical is poured from its container into a wide-mouthed glass vessel, like an old jam-jar, and applied to the workpiece with a brush. After an interval of several minutes, the substance is rubbed off with fine steel wool. Protect your hands by wearing rubber gloves. The surface of the wood is then cleaned with white spirit and allowed to dry thoroughly.

Most treatments of this sort require stringent safety precautions. Always apply the chemical or paste to the workpiece in a well-ventilated area such as on a trestle-table outdoors, or at least close to the open doorway of the workshop, with plenty of old newspapers spread beneath to catch any drips. Do not smoke in the vicinity of the work and be sure to wear hand and eye protectors. If any of the remover accidentally spills on to your skin, wash it off immediately with plenty of water.

FILLING GAPS

No matter how much care you take in measuring and cutting your joints, there are always a few occasions when a gap exists between one piece of wood and another after assembly. This should be minimised as far as possible by cramping up the workpiece very firmly while the glue is still wet. However, you cannot be sure that the lengths of wood are perfectly straight or the joints absolutely square, so small errors do appear.

The finished result will look much better if these gaps are filled. Do not rely on glue to act as a filler, because the modern synthetic adhesives, whilst they do an excellent job of holding the joint rigid, will not absorb wood stain and will, therefore, leave an unsightly mark on the surface of the joint.

Small gaps are filled with a substance known as 'wood stopper'. It is a thick liquid which dries rapidly to form a clay-like paste which can be worked well into the gap with a flexible knife, eventually drying to leave a powdery residue on the surface of the surrounding wood, and a hard mass which holds tenaciously in the gap. After sandpapering flush with the surface of the wood, the stopper accepts wood stain or whatever type of finish you decide to apply.

Wood stoppers are supplied in a range of colours linked to different types of wood. Thus, if you were filling a crack in a mahogany cabinet, you would choose a red-coloured mahogany stopper.

FILLING THE GRAIN

Another point to note is the condition of the grain. For varnishing or polishing, an open grain needs to be filled. Grain filler is available in as many different types and brands as wood stopper, but the method of application is not the same.

A filler is rubbed into the wood with a damp cloth, working across the grain to ensure adequate adhesion. When dry, the filler is sanded smooth with the finest grade of paper. As with the stopper, it is desirable to choose a filler to match as closely as possible to the shade of the wood.

CHANGING THE COLOUR OF THE WOOD

Some pieces of furniture, once thay have been completely assembled and thoroughly rubbed down with sandpaper, are best left in their natural colour. You can tell that they look just right – there is a common tone running throughout and any slight variation serves only to enhance the overall appearance.

There are also plenty of occasions when wood dye must be used to lower the contrast between two or more shades of wood in the same piece of furniture, or to create a completely different colour throughout. For example, most oak furniture is medium or dark brown in colour, but the oak itself is a naturally light-coloured wood, sometimes only marginally darker than ash or beech. There is no definite rule, since the finish is usually a matter of personal choice – although one generally follows an agreed standard, particularly where reproduction styles are concerned.

There are two types of stain in common use; one is water-soluble and the other is dissolved in spirit. The water-soluble stain has the property of penetrating well into the wood, whereas the spirit stain tends to evaporate more quickly, which can prove a slight disadvantage when you are attempting to maintain a wet edge in the staining of a large area.

Whichever stain you choose, the method of application is similar. It can either be poured into a small shallow container – the lid of an old jam-jar is ideal – and applied to the surface of the wood with a soft brush, or you can soak a wad of cotton wool in the stain, wrap this in a clean cotton cloth and rub it on by hand.

The resulting appearance depends on the method used. When you apply the stain with a brush the bristles of the brush soak up a relatively large amount of the liquid and spread it over the surface of the wood in rather a concentrated form. You need to work the brush rapidly if you are to avoid the stain gathering in pools and drying patchily.

It is important to keep a wet edge during the whole of the staining process, which simply means that you commence applying the stain at one end of the piece, usually at one edge, and work progressively along the grain, spreading in an outward direction, so that you never allow the stain to dry completely until you have covered the entire surface. Inevitably, you will have to run the brush back over some of the surface which has already received the stain, working it in long, even strokes. Take care to avoid air bubbles forming on the surface, as these will dry to leave tiny rings.

The alternative method, applying the stain with a soft cotton cloth containing a small wad of cotton wool, ensures a more even distribution of the liquid. Due to the fact that the absorbent cloth does not yield its charge of stain as readily as the brush, you will also find that its effect on the surface of the wood is to leave its colour on the grain to a milder extent.

Stain may be applied to the wood either by brush or cloth. When using a brush, select only a type with the softest bristles. The cloth method similarly requires a soft material, free from fluff.

The first application should be left to dry thoroughly, and then a second rubbing applied, and so on until you have achieved the desired result.

These two contrasting methods leave us with the following conclusion: brush-work is faster than using a cloth because the wood stain goes on to the wood in greater quantity, but unless you are quick and precise with the brush, the resulting finish can appear somewhat blotchy. Rubbing the stain on with the cloth gives you more time to see the effect building up on the wood, and is the better method if you wish to blend together a range of differing tones in the colour of the wood.

When choosing the colour of your wood stain, give some thought to the end result, as there is a wide range of shades available, under different brand-names. For example, if you are using one of the mahoganies or their substitutes, the most appropriate wood dye is the one with a mahogany colour; similarly, teak or afrormosia demand teak-coloured dye. With oak, the choice if not quite so obvious, since the oak stains divide into light, medium and dark. The point to bear in mind is that whichever shade you select, always try it out first on a piece of left-over wood that matches the work-piece, so that you can judge the effect before committing yourself. You may find that the mahogany of one particular manufacturer is just a little too red, or a medium oak is slightly too dark.

The process of staining is always one in which the wood gets progressively darker. However, you will often find that two pieces of material which look identical in texture and natural colour can turn out differently when the stain is applied. This has a most disconcerting effect when they form adjacent parts on the same workpiece, and you end up with one appearing much lighter than the other.

A certain discrepancy can be accepted, but when the colour difference is pronounced, you must aim to bring the two colours closer together. This is where the brush method has the advantage over the cloth method, for as the brush applies a greater amount of stain to the surface, so its colour is more assertive. To achieve the right balance, the answer might be to give the lighter part three applications and the darker part only two, depending on the absorbency of the wood.

End-grain, not surprisingly, is very

absorbent and, consequently, turns out much darker than the surfaces running with the grain. This contrast can be minimised by sealing the end-grain, before staining, with a diluted solution.

APPLYING THE RIGHT FINISH

How do you decide what is the best finish for a particular piece of furniture? Is polyurethane varnish better than French polish, or should the piece be rubbed with an oil or a wax polish? In the end, the choice is largely a matter of personal preference, added to the more practical considerations such as the type and size of furniture, to what use it will be put and whether or not you want to adopt a traditional or a modern finish.

Varnishes

Old-fashioned varnishes were made by dissolving gums and resins in linseed oil, alcohol or water, and were rather slow to dry. By comparison, the modern synthetic polyurethane range of varnishes are easy to apply with a brush, dry fairly quickly, are not so much affected by the surrounding air temperature and give a tough, heat-resisting and waterproof finish which is ideal for furniture in daily use.

Polyurethane varnishes come in three different types, drying to a gloss, satin or matt finish. The same manufacturers also supply a range of coloured varnishes so that you can, up to a point, use them in place of wood dye. If there is a fault with synthetic varnishes, it is the inherent lack of adhesion and penetration into the grain, though this is being steadily im-proved as each successive formula is devised.

Varnishes are applied with a soft, fine-bristled brush, and you may need as many as four coats before a really satisfactory finish is achieved. Each coat is allowed to dry completely, then rubbed down with very fine sandpaper before commencing the next coat. The brush-work must be carried out carefully to avoid creating tiny air bubbles which eventually dry to form craters, and to even out the brush-strokes so that the varnish spreads over the surface in a uniformly smooth covering.

Oils

At one time, the term 'oil' usually referred to the substance known as linseed oil, and was widely used in the treatment of wood to afford it protection and add a shine to the surface. Linseed oil soaks well into the wood and gives a good heat-resisting finish, but its main disadvantage is that it takes a long time to dry.

Teak oil and Danish oil have become very popular. Though both types are referred to collectively, there is a small difference between them. They each have the property of priming, sealing and finishing all woods to leave a soft, lustrous surface which can be used as a basis for varnishing or wax polishing.

Polishes

Wax polish can be applied directly to the wood, either in liquid or cake form, and is perhaps the most satisfactory way of finishing wood, as it can so easily be re-applied at any time. Wax polish is applied to the wood using a soft lint-free

The technique of French polishing demands great skill, and careful preparation of the rubber. It is made from a piece of clean white cotton cloth, which is wrapped around a wad of cotton wool. The French polish is poured on to the cotton wool and the cloth moulded with the fingers into a pear shape until some of the polish soaks through.

cloth and must be rubbed well into the grain. It cannot be too strongly emphasised that the more effort that is put into the rubbing action, the better the shine. Some polishes are specially blended for light woods, whilst others have a deeper tone.

French polish creates a much more refined appearance than any other type of wood treatment, resulting in an almost glass-like surface with a high reflectiveness. The drawback is that it demands great skill in its application. The polish is made from shellac dissolved in methy-

lated spirits or, more usually, polyurethane. A few drops of the liquid are poured on to a wad of cotton wool and this is wrapped in a piece of muslin or cotton cloth, and the gathered ends of the cloth twisted to form a pear shape. This 'rubber', as it is called, is then worked over the surface of the workpiece in a circular motion until every part of it has been covered.

The rubber must not be allowed to dry out, otherwise you will scuff the polish which has already been applied and ruin the smoothness. When the first applica-

A wad of very fine wire wool.

tion has dried thoroughly, rub down the entire surface gently with very fine steel wool or sandpaper. Brush off the particles of dust and apply a further coat, continuing until four or five rubbings have been performed. The last application is carried out by working the rubber in the direction of the grain, and the result is a high-quality gloss finish which can later be given a wax polish to maintain the shine.

French polish will not stand up to everyday use, so great care must be taken to protect those pieces of furniture to which it has been applied.

8   Butt Joints

A butt joint is formed when the squared and planed edges or sides of two pieces of wood are brought together, or the edge of one piece and the side of the other. Although the butt joint is the simplest means of effecting a join between two pieces of wood, this most basic of joints has the ability to turn up in many different shapes and sizes according to circumstances.

The main point in its favour is the ease with which it can be made. Being a surface joint, in which two flat faces or edges are butted up against each other, it is unique in that it cannot be fitted together; the abutment between the two parts only allows for the joint to be laid in position.

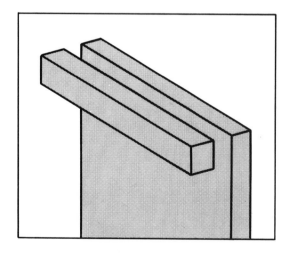

Exploded butt joint.

TYPICAL APPLICATIONS

Its apparent simplicity might lead you to think that the butt joint does not have many uses in furniture-making. It is interesting to consider, however, that some of the finest work to emerge from the hands of the skilled cabinet-maker has depended for its success on the butt joint. That is the process of veneering, in which a thin layer of high-class wood is laid on a flat surface comprising of a less distinguished species which forms the carcase of the piece.

The butt joint rarely makes a direct contribution to the main construction of the furniture, but often takes a supporting role. Two such examples are the triangular corner joining block employed to reinforce the attachment of the rails to the legs of a chair, or a drawer runner used to support a sliding cupboard drawer.

In other forms, it is the butt joint that fixes a piece of moulding to the surface or edge to add decorative effect to the finished piece.

METHODS OF PREPARATION

Preparation of the butt joint is limited to cutting the wood to size and planing the surfaces to be joined until they are perfectly flat and thus able to make complete

The side or edge of the wood must be planed perfectly flat to make for a successful butt joint.

contact with each other. It is usual for both the joining surfaces to lie in the same direction as the grain, such as two boards butted edge-to-edge, or the edge of one butted up against the face of the other, in which case the pieces may either be held firmly in the vice or clamped to the top of the work-bench whilst the surfaces are planed flat.

With corner joining blocks, the arrangement is somewhat different, since the triangular shape of each block means that it is not possible for both the joining edges to follow the direction of the grain. In fact, it is common practice for the grain to run with the base of the triangle, so that the two adjacent edges that are used to butt up against the two rails of a chair or table construction are cut at an angle to the grain. For a right-angled corner, both angles will be at 45 degrees to the grain. For a corner block used to join the top of a cabinet to its frame, the blocks are cut lengthwise and split or sawn into the appropriate triangles so that each of the three faces lies equally with the grain.

I would not recommend that you attempt a butt joint with end-grain. There are three reasons for this. To begin with, there are very few circumstances in which end-grain actually calls for a butt joint; secondly, end-grain represents the cross-sectional area of the wood which, compared with its faces and edges, is very small and, therefore, offers minimal potential to create a practical joint; and, thirdly, end-grain at the best of times is difficult to plane perfectly flat without roughing up the edges.

Once the joining surfaces have been cut to size and planed smooth, the next task is to bring them together to form a permanent fixture. There are various ways of making the joint secure. In cabinet work, the butt joint is nearly always put together with glue. However, there are occasions when some additional or alternative method of fixing is required. By 'additional', I am referring to a means of reinforcing the effectiveness of the wood glue; an 'alternative' method, on the other hand, does away with the need for glue, and, therefore, implies a butt joint which is effected with screws or nails and may, consequently, be dismantled at some later stage without causing damage to the surrounding wood.

ASSEMBLING WITH GLUE

This method will only succeed if the wood glue has sufficient strength to retain its hold on both joining surfaces, and provided those surfaces are of a large enough area over which it can act. Any inherently weak glue spread over an area that is too small will not make for a good butt joint.

The procedure is quite straightforward: once the wood glue has been mixed to the correct consistency, it is applied with a brush to both the joining surfaces. It is not necessary to spread the glue thickly, because this will not make the joint any stronger. On the contrary, too much glue can often be a hindrance because it will cause the two parts of the joint to slide against each other during assembly.

When the glue has turned slightly tacky, bring the joining surfaces together in the required position, and hold them under firm pressure for a period of time whilst the glue gradually dries and hardens. Clamps or cramps are normally used for this purpose. However, there can be times when the joint is used in some rather obscure location where clamps could not possibly reach, in which case some alternative method must be found to apply the necessary pressure.

Never be afraid to resort to such heavyweight objects as bricks, for these are an ideal way of keeping two joining surfaces in close contact. But be sure that they are completely dry, because bricks have a tendency to retain moisture even when they have been kept indoors for a period, and any dampness will find its way on to the wood. It is advisable to place a barrier between the brick and the workpiece – this can be a wad of old newspaper or an off-cut of scrap wood. For smaller joints which need little pressure to keep their surfaces in contact, a couple of heavy books are suitable.

As with all glued assembly work, some of the glue will probably squeeze out when the pressure is applied, leaving a thin trail around the edge of the joint. Indeed, this is a good sign because it indicates that the two joining surfaces have been brought into close contact. If an inspection of the assembly reveals no glue at all, this is a useful indication that you have either not applied enough glue to the joint or, more likely, that the surfaces are not making contact. When the trail of glue is intermittent, this is even more damning evidence that you have not planed the surfaces perfectly flat!

If you consider that the joint is being held by glue and nothing else, then the absence of any squeezed-out glue should be sufficient to tell you that the joint ought to be dismantled again, before it is too late, to find the cause. It is good practice to remove all traces of surplus glue by wiping it away with a clean, damp cloth, but take care not to move the joint out of position in doing so.

Certain types of wood glue, when they have completely hardened, make a very strong bond indeed, and it is often said that the resulting joint possesses greater strength than the surrounding wood. This can easily be proved true with some glues by making a prototype butt joint, using the same materials as for the proper joint. After the glue has fully cured, you will discover that if you try to separate the two parts of the joint, the adjoining wood will splinter before the joint itself surrenders.

Assembling with Screws

For butt joints which involve large sections of wood which are subject to constant or heavy loads, it is usual to reinforce the glue with woodscrews. There will be times when you do not want the joint to be permanent, as in the case of the runners for a drawer. These have a habit of wearing down with prolonged use, and might well need replacing at some future time. It would be so much simpler to take off the old runners and fit new ones if the wood could be unscrewed without the inevitable breakage that occurs when trying to separate a glued joint. The detachable butt joint is normally fitted together with woodscrews in preference to nails, assuming that the screw-thread passes perpendicularly to the direction of the grain, and not in the same direction.

When the security of the joint depends on screws and nothing else, pay particular attention to the size of screw used, its length and the number that are employed over the length of the joint, for these three factors each have an important bearing on its strength. Considering the size of the screw first, you are always advised to use the largest possible. Where the head of the screw is out of sight, such as on the inside or undersurface of a cabinet, this presents no real problem, for however big the head should be it will not be seen.

There are ways of concealing the head from view, but this supposes that it is being placed on an external surface – which is not good practice. However, if it cannot be avoided, the hole for the screw may be countersunk a little deeper than the surface and once the screw has been driven into position, the space above the head filled with a suitable compound which is capable of being sandpapered smooth and painted over with wood stain to produce a stopping which is barely visible. Indeed, the screw may be set even further down into the wood so that the hole above it can be plugged with a short length of wooden dowelling. Finally, the surface of the wood may sometimes be lifted in a small flap and raised out of the way until the screw has been fitted, and then glued back down. This last form of concealment is frequently restricted to hiding nails, which have smaller heads, and obviously the wood must possess a high degree of spring to it, otherwise it will splinter off.

The number 8 screw size is a useful all-rounder, and finds a place in most furniture construction. Where the two joining pieces of wood are particularly large, or the stresses placed upon the joint are high, it is wise to opt for a size such as number 10 or perhaps number 12. Conversely, small sections of wood which are subject to smaller loadings will find the number 6 size quite adequate. These numbers relate to the diameter of the screw's shank and thread.

The length of the screw, which is a measurement of the depth to which it sinks in the wood, is quoted either in inches or millimetres. The length is divided into three parts, comprising: the head, which is either countersunk or rounded; the smooth shank which immediately adjoins the head; and the screw-thread, which tapers gradually to a point at the tip of the screw. If you examine the shank and the screw-thread carefully, you will see that the shank has a greater diameter than the screw-thread when you ignore the spiral screw pattern and concentrate only on the shaft at its centre.

Normally, you select a drill bit to match the size of the screw, such as a number 6, 8 or 10, which bores the hole to give sufficient clearance for the shank to pass easily into the first piece of wood, but then reduces in diameter so that the further it goes into the second piece, the smaller the hole becomes to leave sufficient wood for the screw-thread to take a firm hold. Before commencing the hole you should measure the length of the screw and set this amount on the drill-bit, using a piece of sticky tape as a depth-guide. Clamp the two parts of the joint together in their assembled position and drill out the hole until the bit sinks down to the guide-mark. To fit a countersunk screw, remove the drill bit from the handbrace and replace it with a countersinking cutter, making a cone on the surface of the wood to the required size.

The usual method of choosing the screw length is to measure the combined thicknesses of the two pieces of wood to be joined, and pick the next size down so

that the screw, when fitted, remains well hidden within the wood and does not break through the opposite surface.

In practice, this can present difficulties, especially when the first piece of wood – that is to say, the piece which receives the head and the shank – is particularly deep, and the second piece, into which the screw-thread passes, is very shallow by comparison.

One example of a situation where this can occur is when a table top is fitted to a frame which has deep top rails. Several solutions are possible. Clearly, this is a form of butt joint in which glue would be virtually useless. The first, and perhaps the most difficult, is to use a technique known as pocket screwing, in which a curved notch is gouged on the inside face of the rail, somewhere near its upper edge, so that a much shorter screw can be accommodated.

Pocket screwing.

Second, metal fixing brackets can be screwed to both of the joining surfaces. This method has a positive advantage, because certain types of right-angled bracket have enlarged holes which permit the wood to expand or contract without causing it to split, since any movement is absorbed by the bracket. This is very useful when fixing a large area of wood, such as a table top, on to its frame.

The third solution is to fit corner blocks which are not nearly as deep as the rails, and serve an additional purpose to strengthen the frame. Corner blocks are triangular pieces of wood, usually cut from off-cut material, which have right-angled edges that butt up against the two rails to be joined. The rails themselves are attached to a leg or post usually with a dowel or mortise and tenon joints, and it is not uncommon for a square notch to be cut at the apex of the triangular-shaped block to fit around the leg. A single screw is driven through each of the two adjacent right-angled edges and thus into the inside faces of the rails. Glue is also applied to the joining surfaces.

For the majority of work, you can use mild steel woodscrews which are strong and will not rust on interior furniture. However, certain woods contain substances which react with the iron in these screws to leave a distinctive blue colour on the surface of the wood. Oak is a classic example. To avoid this stain from occurring, brass screws should be used instead of those made from mild steel.

There is one drawback – brass is a relatively soft alloy and does not possess the same strength as steel. When the screw is being driven into its drilled hole for the first time, there is always the chance that it might shear, especially with the smaller sizes such as number 6 or less. The best advice is to use a mild steel screw of exactly the same size and length to cut the initial thread, then remove it from the hole and fit an equivalent brass screw in its place.

Assembling with Nails

Nails do not play a very prominent role in cabinet-making, and when they do occur it is often in support of the butt joint.

Decorative mouldings are normally abutted to the edge of the workpiece in some position such as a cornice, and whilst it would be true to say that wood glue has ample strength to make a lasting joint, it is commonplace to affix the moulding with tiny veneer or panel pins in addition to glue. The heads of the pins are driven down into the wood with a small punch so that they are completely out of sight, and the resulting holes filled with wood stopper.

9 Dowel Joints

The dowel joint can take several forms, but in general it is similar to the butt joint except that it is precisely located and fastened by one or more lengths of wooden dowelling.

The purpose of the dowel, or peg, is to serve as a fixing pin which is glued to both parts of the joint and thus locates them permanently in place. It has two important functions. First, it holds the joint firm against any tendency to pull apart, and second, it prevents the two joining surfaces from sliding laterally.

Since the dowels serve to reinforce what amounts to a simple butt joint, the overall effect is to secure the two pieces of wood doubly (the butt joint taking effect by having glue applied along the entire joining surfaces). In theory, therefore, the dowel joint offers potential for great strength. If the dowels only were to be glued, then the strength of the resulting joint would depend merely on the cross-sectional area of the dowels, which is small compared with the joint's total area.

The dowel joint is often regarded as one of the more recent innovations in woodwork, acting as a substitute for the mortise and tenon in many contemporary designs, but it does actually have a long history of use. It was employed in some of the earliest types of furniture before the nail had been developed, and so was the forerunner of the nail and screw.

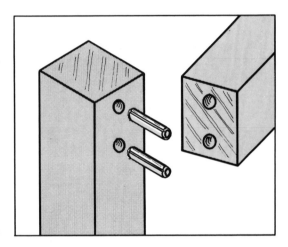

Exploded dowel joint.

TYPICAL APPLICATIONS

As with any other type of joint, the dowel joint always poses an important question for the cabinet-maker: what are the most appropriate circumstances for its use, and will it prove strong enough for the job?

The answer, of course, lies in what we are aiming to achieve. The fact that a furniture manufacturer uses dowels to join together the frame of a table or chair should certainly not be taken as a general recommendation for use, when it is obvious that the best sort of joint for this type of construction is the mortise and tenon. Similarly, you will encounter table tops which have been made up from several narrow boards, all dowel-jointed

A series of dowels has been used in the construction of this cabinet carcase.

edge-to-edge. A more superior result would be expected if the boards had been assembled with housing joints, known more commonly as tongued-and-grooved joints, running continuously along the entire length of the edges.

On the other hand, the dowel joint can be very useful to get you out of a tight spot. In a cabinet construction involving the fitting of internal divisions or partitions, the dowels may be set in the edge of the dividing panels at the various points where they meet the framework. Indeed, this can be extended to take in the side panels themselves, where they need to be joined effectively to a top and base panel. Having said that, it is usual in such a case for the top and base to be additionally joined together with upright posts, one at every corner, and these should be assembled with mortise and tenon joints.

Even allowing for its shortcomings, the dowel joint is still most versatile and will serve you well, whether as a substitute for the mortise and tenon, as a means of strengthening a housing joint, or simply to join the long edge of one piece to the face of another. It can be used with equal success to join end-grain to cross-grain, unlike nails and screws which favour either one or the other, and, as dowels come in various diameters, it can be applied both to narrow edges or wide faces with ease.

DOWELLING MATERIAL

Before going on to describe in more detail how dowel joints are prepared, we must first consider the material from which the dowelling is made. In theory, of course, it can be any wood, since there is nothing to stop you from making your own dowels. To do so, you will need to make two special tools – a wooden cradle and a metal dowel cutter. The cradle is simply two identical lengths of chamfered wood screwed together side by side so that the chamfers meet to form a V-shaped channel with a triangular piece of wood glued at one end to act as a stop. It enables you to lay square-sectioned lengths of wood flat to have their corners planed into an octagonal configuration. For small-diameter dowelling, you will require a shallow cradle, whereas for larger diameters the V-shaped trough will have to be deeper. It helps to make several cradles to suit a range of diameters.

The metal dowel cutter is a sheet of ¼in (6mm)-thick metal plate in which a number of holes have been drilled with a metal-cutting bit equal in diameter to that of the dowelling – for instance ¼in (6mm), ⅜in (9mm), ½in (13mm) and so on. Having planed the wood to an octagon slightly larger than the size of dowelling you want, place the end of the wood over the selected hole in the metal plate and hammer it through. As it emerges on the other side, you should have a perfect rod of dowel. When the material has nearly passed through the metal plate, cut it off with the hacksaw and drive out the small amount of waste with a small nail to avoid damaging the plate with the hammer. By making your own dowels, you can choose whatever wood you want.

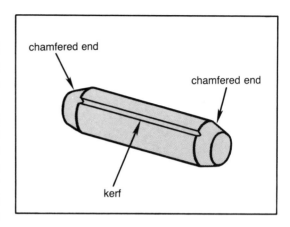

A fully prepared dowel, with chamfered ends and a glue channel sawn along its length.

Dowels are sold commercially in long lengths covering a range of standard diameters, and are usually made from the light-coloured hardwood ramin. The most common sizes are ¼in (6mm), ⅜in (9mm), ½in (13mm), ⅝in (16mm) and ¾in (19mm). Occasionally you will find a slight discrepancy between the diameter of the dowel material and the drill bit, giving you a dowel that is either much too loose in its hole or too big to fit.

It makes sense to carry out a trial run on a piece of scrap wood before you begin preparing your dowel joints in the workpiece. Ideally, the dowel should slide into its hole with no more than firm pressure from the fingers.

METHODS OF PREPARATION

I have already mentioned that the dowel joint has a wide range of applications, but these may be divided into two main categories: there are those joints which are made by bringing together two edges or sides, where both parts run in the same direction as the grain; and there are the joints in which the end-grain of one piece is brought up against the edge or side of the other.

As typical examples of these two groups, think of joining together two planks side-by-side to form a panel, such as a table top or side panel for a cabinet, as a representative of the first category; and the construction of a framework in which rails are joined to legs, or similar arrangements, as representing the second. You will probably be able to think of further applications, but mostly they will fall within two groups. It is comparatively rare to use the dowel joint for end-grain to end-grain, although it does provide you with a convenient method of repairing broken legs in old furniture, so I will look at this briefly on page 98.

Whichever type of dowel joint is to be employed, the first important step is to prepare the abutting surfaces of both pieces so that they meet perfectly, much as if you were making ordinary butt joints. Even the most carefully prepared wood is not always absolutely straight and true. In the case of a side or edge running in the same direction as the grain, this means planing the surface perfectly flat. For end-grain, the wood must be squared around with the pencil and try-square, and sawn perpendicularly with the edge. Only a fine-toothed saw blade should be used, to avoid scuffing the top and bottom edges of the end-grain. This means either a tenon saw with at least sixteen points to the inch or a high-speed electric jigsaw fitted with a fine-cutting blade.

When the end-grain has to be prepared accurately across the width of a large board, such as that forming the side panel of a cabinet, it is not always easy to guarantee that the saw cut is perfectly straight and square for the full length of the cut. When a dowel joint needs to be prepared along such an end-grain, the normal procedure is to plane it square and flat with the smoothing plane or the electric plane, taking the usual precautions.

Test that both parts of the joint butt fully against one another, so that if they are held firmly in position there is no tendency to wobble. When the joint is to run along the edges of two long boards, a high degree of planing skill is required to ensure that the edges come into contact all the way from one end to the other.

JOINING TWO EDGES OR SIDES

There are a number of circumstances when this method is applied, and it would be unrealistic to give a detailed account for each particular case. The most common instance is when joining together two or more planks to make up a board. I have already mentioned that dowel joints are not the most perfect means for an edge-to-edge assembly, but for reasons of speed or simplicity there are occasions when this is the preferred method. Individual planks or boards used for making up wide panels are frequently planed to a thickness of ¾in (19mm), and this is a very convenient size.

One of the most important factors governing the success of the dowel joint is to select the most appropriate size of dowel in relation to the thickness of the wood. It must not be too small to deprive it of the necessary strength, nor must it be too large for it to be placed close to the surface of the wood and thus risk causing splits to occur. A ⅜in (9mm) diameter dowel is the correct choice, giving a margin of ³⁄₁₆ (5mm) on either side. Plane the joining edges straight and square so that they abutt perfectly along the length of the joint.

Set the marking gauge so that its spur makes a line half-way across the thickness of the two boards, and scribe the line along the entire length of each abutting edge. As there is often a very slight discrepancy between the path of the marking gauge's spur and the absolute mid-point of the edge, it is important that you mark both lines from the face side for both boards. That is to say, in each case work the gauge with its fence bearing against the two upper surfaces or lower surfaces rather than a mixture of the two, thus ensuring that any minor error is automatically compensated.

Measure and mark the centre of each dowel hole along both lines. Clearly you will have to decide how frequently you locate a dowel, and this decision partly depends on the use to which the finished

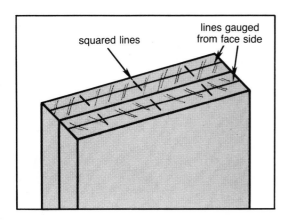

The two boards are placed side by side and the dowel positions marked.

jointed board will be put. Intervals of between 6–8in (150–200mm) are appropriate in most cases. Mark the centre of each hole position in pencil, squaring across the edge from the face side. It should then be possible to place the two pieces of wood side-by-side and check with the square that all the marked positions are in perfect alignment.

Clamp the first board in the vice with its jointing edge facing uppermost, and drill out all the holes using a ⅜in (9mm) diameter centre bit mounted in the handbrace. Bore each hole to a depth of 1in (25mm). As the drill bit enters the wood, it should be at right-angles to the edge; this can easily be tested with the square. When all the holes have been drilled in the first piece, remove it from the vice and repeat the same procedure with the second board.

The total depth of each combined dowel hole is 2in (50mm), but the dowels must be slightly shorter if they are to be assembled successfully, to allow for fragments of wood drillings which often get trapped at the bottom of the hole, together with a certain amount of glue. A dowel length of 1¾in (44mm) is correct in this case. Count up the total number that you need, measure and mark them off along a strip of dowelling material measuring ⅜in (9mm) in diameter, and cut them to length with the hacksaw.

Chamfer the ends of each dowel slightly by giving it a few twists in a pencil sharpener. Only the smaller diameter dowels can be trimmed in this way; larger sizes must be pared with a chisel. The effect of this chamfering is to reduce the diameter at both ends so that the dowel enters its drilled holes more easily. The saw should also be run along the length of each individual dowel a few

Each board is clamped in the vice, and a series of holes drilled along the joining edges with the handbrace and a suitable-sized drill bit.

times so that the kerf forms a shallow groove for the glue to squeeze up into during assembly, rather than becoming trapped in an air pocket at the bottom of the hole. One further trick which may be employed is to fit the countersinking bit in the handbrace and slightly chamfer the top of each hole, so that any accumulated glue can gather and give a little extra strength to the joint.

Before final assembly, make a test-fitting of the dowels in their holes to check that they all align. When you are satisfied that all is well, mix a quantity of wood glue. It is always difficult to estimate the amount you need, but remember that glue must be applied to both the edges as well as the dowel holes. It is better to make a little too much than to

run out half-way through the assembling process.

Taking a small artist's paintbrush, apply the glue thoroughly to both the joining surfaces of the two boards, and work it well into the drilled holes. With the first board held in the vice, brush some of the glue on to the individual dowels and fit them into their holes along its edge. Finger pressure should be sufficient to locate them within each hole. Now bring the second board into position, align the upper ends of all the dowels with their corresponding holes – the chamfering of the dowels and the holes makes this a quick and easy operation – and tap the two boards together with the mallet.

When knocking together any joint, it is advisable to place a piece of clean scrap

The joint is glued together. Glue is applied by brush to the lengths of dowel,
their receiver holes and the two abutting surfaces.

wood between the mallet and the work-piece, to ensure that the blows do not dent the wood. It is very important to use only clean wood for this purpose, such as an off-cut of the same material with a good, straight edge. Do not strike it with a single heavy blow, but make a number of gentle taps along the full length of the joint until all the dowels have fitted fully into their holes.

Check both sides of the assembled joint to make sure that it has fitted together as you intended, with no gaps between the two boards. Cramp up the assembly using two or more sash cramps, applying a firm, even pressure along the length of the joint. As the cramps gradually tighten, so a small amount of glue will squeeze out from the joint and leave a trail on both surfaces. This indicates that the two joining edges

have come completely together. Remove the glue by wiping the surfaces with a clean cloth moistened with lukewarm water.

Place the assembly to one side for a period specificed by the glue manufacturer, and when the indicated time has elapsed, remove the cramps.

JOINTING END-GRAIN TO EDGE OR SIDE

With this type of dowel joint, the end-grain is usually, but not always, restricted in terms of its area, since it invariably represents the end of a rail which needs to be joined to a leg or a post. It is used in a door construction to join the horizontal rail to the vertical stile. There are those rare cases when you are recommended to use the dowel joint to assemble the side panel of a cabinet to a top and bottom panel, in which case the method is much the same, except that the end-grain extends over a considerably greater length.

If we examine a typical end-grain to edge dowel joint comprising of a rail to leg assembly, as you might find in the construction of a small table framework, the method of making all other types should follow suit. Once again, the joining surfaces must be well prepared, with the edge of the leg planed perfectly flat and smooth, and the end-grain of the rail cut and planed square.

Mark in the positions of the dowels. For the end-grain of the rail, set the spur of the marking gauge to coincide with the mid-point across the thickness of the material and scribe a line along it, working the gauge from the face side. The leg is marked likewise, once the rail position has been marked in with a square and pencil. However, it is often the case that the leg is of greater thickness than the rail, and it does not necessarily follow that you want to place the rail centrally across its edge. Adjust the spur of the gauge until it sets the centre of the rail to the desired position on the edge of the leg, and scribe the line between the squared pencil markings.

Some thought must be given to the size of the dowels to be used, and this will depend on the smaller of the two jointing surfaces which is normally the end-grain. Aim to leave a distance of ¼in (6mm) between the hole and the two sides of the rail, and a similar gap between the hole and the edge. At least two dowels must be used to make a secure joint – it is rarely necessary to use three, unless the rail is particularly wide.

Measure the centre of the dowel hole positions on the end-grain using the tape-measure and pencil, and adjust the two spurs of the mortise gauge to coincide with these marks. The fence should be adjusted so that it bears against the face edge. By the simple task of making one or two strokes with the gauge, you will find that the centre of the two dowel holes is clearly marked on the end-grain. Lining up the rail with the leg, mark off the gauged positions on the leg in pencil, and square across the scribed line.

An alternative to this method is to cut out a thick card template equal in size to the end-grain of the rail, and mark the two dowel hole positions by pushing the point of the bradawl through. When this same template is used for both the end-grain of the rail and the edge of the leg, you are assured of accuracy between the two settings.

Drill out the two holes in the edge of the leg, boring down to a depth of at least 1in (25mm), and more if possible. Ideally, the depth should equal approximately three-quarters the width of the piece. Now clamp the rail upright in the vice, and drill down into the end-grain. To make a good start, tap the point of the bradawl into the two marked positions, so that the tip of the drill-bit has a pilot-hole to start it off. Drilling into end-grain is always more difficult than boring across the grain, because there is a tendency for the drill bit to drift. To avoid this, you should use a bit that has a long spiral shaft. Drill to a depth approximately equal to that of the leg holes.

Using a depth-gauge, measure the combined depths of both holes, and cut two pieces of dowelling slightly less, chamfering the ends and running a saw kerf along their length. Countersink the surface of the holes, mix some wood glue, and apply it to the dowels, their holes and the two joining surfaces.

Often, the dowel joint used in these circumstances forms part of an overall assembly, where a number of joints are all put together at the same time in the construction of a frame. When the assembly is complete, hold it firmly in place with cramps until the glue has dried and set hard.

JOINING END-GRAIN TO END-GRAIN

Although this does not arise very often, it must be mentioned, as a third method. There are occasions, usually involving the repair of an existing piece of furniture, when a leg may need to be sawn to remove a part that is badly infested with woodworm. Indeed, you may even discover an old item which has a set of attractive barley-twist legs which you wish to dismantle so that the twists can be used on a new piece of furniture.

When part of the leg must be cut and joined to a new section of matching wood, the preferred method is to use the single dowel. Mark the existing piece of leg with the square and pencil, and cut off the unwanted portion. Then plane up a length of new wood to take the place of the damaged or worm-eaten wood, preparing it to exactly the same dimensions. Square off the end, and cut with the saw so that it butts up perfectly against the end of the good barley-twist section, or whatever piece you wish to use. We now have a situation where two pieces of wood need to be jointed end-grain to end-grain.

With a pencil and ruler, draw two lines between the opposite corners of each end-grain, so that they cross at the centre. Tap the point of the bradawl at the place where these two lines intersect, then clamp the pieces one at a time in the vice and drill down with a ½in (13mm) or ⅝in (16mm) drill bit, whichever is more appropriate for the size of the wood. Bore to a depth of at least 1½in (38mm) per hole, and cut the dowelling to a length of 2⅞in (72mm). Trim the ends of the dowel with a chisel, and run the blade of the tenon saw along its length to make a glue channel.

Mix some glue, apply it thoroughly to both parts of the joint, and to the surface of the dowel, and bring the two parts together. Pressure should be applied with a single sash cramp until the glue has set hard.

10 Mitre Joints

The mitre joint is formed by two pieces of wood with their ends cut at an angle of 45 degrees so that they meet to form a right-angled corner. The angle may be varied to suit different types of work calling for larger or smaller angles, but the 90-degree mitre joint remains the most common.

In its simplest form, the two parts of the mitre joint are butted up together and assembled with wood glue, but as the area of the joining surface is rather limited, this method does not offer great strength and is only suitable if the joint is not intended to receive any stresses or strains. In circumstances where such loadings are likely to be encountered, the joint can be reinforced by several techniques, such as nailing together from both directions, or adding dowels, keys and false tenons.

TYPICAL APPLICATIONS

In cabinet-making, we usually associate the mitre joint with adding decorative mouldings to the external surfaces of the piece, whether it might be a thin cornice moulding at the top of a cupboard, or when assembling wide boards to create the effect of a plinth at the base of a column.

Of course, there are other uses for the mitre joint. It can be employed to construct a square or rectangular frame for a simple door, or to join together the sides and back of a drawer – though in both these cases there are other joints that are normally preferred, unless you have an

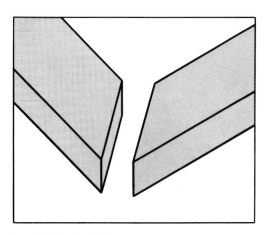

Exploded mitre joint.

A typical example of the mitre joint is in forming a right-angled corner between two pieces of decorative moulding.

important reason for keeping them as straightforward as possible, like the building of miniature furniture for a doll's house.

It is rarely a good idea to use the mitre joint in the main structure of a frame or cabinet carcase, but you will find it a useful adjunct to the mortise and tenon joint where two tenons meet inside a leg or post and need to have their ends mitred so that the two adjoining mortises can accommodate them satisfactorily.

METHODS OF PREPARATION

The Simple Mitre

There are two ways of preparing the simple mitre, which consists of no more than two lengths of wood with a 45-degree angle cut at one end. The first method is to measure out the position where each of the two angled cuts is to be made on its respective piece of wood, and mark across with a mitre square, which has its blade set at an angle of 45 degrees. Square across the two edges, and repeat the angle on the opposite side, always working from face side and face edge. Clamp the piece to the side of the work-bench, or hold it in the bench hook, and cut off the waste with the tenon saw. The angled cut can then be trimmed by placing the wood on a mitre shooting board and planing it smooth with the ordinary plane.

The second method starts the same way, measuring the position of the joint on both lengths of wood, but, instead of marking with the mitre square, the two

The 45° mitres are usually prepared by marking the angles on the wood and then sawing in the mitre box.

pieces are cut immediately by placing them one at a time in a mitre box, lining them up with the 45-degree saw guides, and cutting them with the tenon saw. In either instance, you rely for accuracy on the use of a special jig – the shooting board or the mitre box. Both of these can be bought, or you can make your own.

The simple mitre joint can be used as it stands, with the two parts glued together as with cornice moulding, or it can form the basis of all subsequent variations.

THE DOWELLED MITRE

Start by making a simple mitre, and combine this with the method of preparing the dowel joint to insert two lengths of dowelling into the two abutting ends. The main complication with this type of reinforcement is that the dowel nearer to the tip of the joint must necessarily be very short, and you will have to carry out the drilling with great care to prevent the bit from splitting through the outer edge of both pieces. The longer of the two dowels does not present a problem, because there is plenty of wood in which the hole can be drilled.

The drilling itself calls for the bit to be worked at right-angles to the mitred ends. Check that it is exactly perpendicular with the square. Cut the dowels to length and glue them in their holes as you would for a normal dowel joint.

THE KEYED MITRE

The keyed mitre offers greater strength and probably less risk than the dowelled

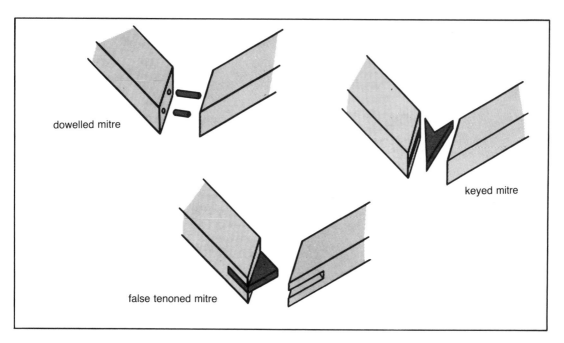

dowelled mitre

keyed mitre

false tenoned mitre

The abutting surfaces of the mitre joint can be strengthened with dowels, the use of a key, or a false tenon.

mitre. It consists of a slot cut in each mitred end into which a shaped wooden key is fitted. The slot extends for the full length of the end, but gets progressively deeper as it approaches the inner edge of the piece. Its width should be equal to one-third the thickness of the wood, and is marked with the mortise gauge, the spurs and fence adjusted so that the two parallel lines score centrally along the thickness.

Clamp the two pieces one at a time in the vice and cut out the slots with the tenon saw, completing the work with the chisel. The key is shaped like the point of an arrow, its tip coinciding with the outside corner of the joint, and its base given a squared notch which aligns with the inside right-angle.

The key is equal in thickness to the width of the slot. It is glued in place and the two parts of the joint are held together with corner clamps while the glue sets.

THE FALSE TENONED MITRE

This is merely an extension of the keyed mitre, but this time the key, or false tenon, takes the form of a square piece of wood set into two triangular slots which, when combined, equal the size of the square thus formed. As with the arrow-shaped key, the false tenon is glued in position.

11 Housing Joints

The housing joint is formed by fitting the end of one piece into a groove cut along the length, or across the grain, of the second piece so that when the two parts are brought together they result in a recessed right-angled joint.

The simplest type of housing joint consists of a groove whose width is equal to the thickness of the board that fits into it. The groove may either run for the full width of the piece in which it is cut, so that the recessed board is visible along both edges, or it can be stopped. When the groove occurs at the end of the wood and resembles a rebate, the housing now takes the form of a lapped joint.

Other variations are possible. For instance, the groove may be cut to a width less than the thickness of the board and shoulders cut along the end of the board to fit into it, making a more rigid assembly. A dovetailed housing joint offers even greater strength, as once the two parts are slid into position they cannot be pulled apart.

The housing joint is usually clearly defined, and therefore easy to recognise, but when it takes the form of a stopped groove cut in the first piece of wood, with a matching set of shoulders cut in the second piece that fits into the groove, you could well be forgiven for calling this a stopped four-shouldered mortise and tenon joint. There are such occasions when it is difficult to make the distinction between one joint and another, but when you are faced with having to decide which type to use for a particular application, it does not matter what name you give to it, so long as it serves its purpose.

TYPICAL APPLICATIONS

The housing joint has such a wide range of applications that it is no wonder it is of great importance to the cabinet-maker. Whenever you need to cut a groove or a rebate, this usually signifies the presence of a housing joint.

The classic instance of fitting a board into a groove is in the design and construction of a bookcase, where upright panels are grooved across their width to receive the ends of several shelves. A similar arrangement is favoured in many other types of cabinet work where a back panel has to be set inside grooves cut in a standard carcase assembly consisting of a

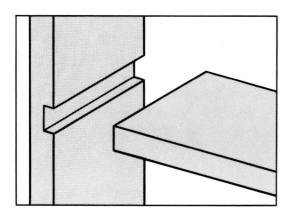

Exploded housing joint.

top, back and two side members; then there are cases where side panels are mounted in rebates cut in a framework assembly. A less obvious variant, but a housing joint nonetheless, is fitting a plywood panel into grooves cut on the inside edge of a cabinet door frame.

METHODS OF PREPARATION

The Plain Housing Joint

To make a plain housing joint, take the piece of wood in which the groove is to be cut and check that its surface is perfectly flat. The board that fits into the groove must have its end marked and cut square, and the end-grain cleaned up with the plane.

Measure the thickness of the board as accurately as possible, and use this distance to set the width of the groove, squaring across the surface of the wood and scribing two parallel lines with the blade of the marking knife. Continue the marking of the lines around both edges in pencil.

Depending on the thickness of the wood in which the groove is to be cut, the depth of the groove should be half the thickness, or less, of the piece. Set the marking gauge to the required distance, and scribe a line on both edges between the two squared width lines. Make sure you work the gauge from the face side on each occasion.

Clamp the piece firmly to the top of the work-bench, and make two saw cuts with the tenon saw, keeping the blade on the waste side of the two lines. Saw down as far as the depth lines. Remove the waste with the chisel and mallet,

working from one edge and then the other so that the chisel cuts meet half-way across the width of the wood. A quick and effective alternative to cutting out the groove by hand is to work it with the electric router. The diameter of the cutter should be less than the required width of the groove, and two or three passes made within the marked-out area, using a length of straight-edged batten to act as a guide for the tool. If the groove runs in the same direction as the grain, the groove could be cut with the plough plane.

When all the waste has been removed, fit the end of the board into its groove. The two parts should fit together with firm hand pressure.

The joint is secured with wood glue, but it may also be strengthened with dowels or nails. If dowels are used, you will need to prepare a dowel joint between the two abutting surfaces, marking and drilling out a series of corresponding dowel holes. Nails can be driven straight in through the back of the groove so that they take hold in the end-grain of the board. Nails, however, are recommended in only the rarest of circumstances.

The Stopped Housing Joint

Instead of the groove running across the entire width of the wood as in the case of the plain housing joint, a stopped groove finishes before it reaches one or both edges of the piece. The method of marking differs because the stopped end is set in from the edge by some pre-arranged amount, and, therefore, its depth cannot be marked on the edge with the gauge. The most suitable tool for cutting a stopped groove is the router, because its

Method of cutting groove for the housing joint across the grain. Shoulder lines are scored with the marking knife, and shallow channels cut with the chisel. Saw cuts are made along the two lines, down as far as the scribed depth line.

The waste is chopped out with the chisel to form the groove. The chisel is worked first from one edge of the wood and then the other, so as not to cause splits at the end.

The quickest way of preparing the groove, either with or across the grain, is to employ the electric router, which produces a neater and more precise result. However, you must guide the passage of the router with great care, using a length of straight-edged batten clamped to the surface of the workpiece.

depth can be set before the cut is commenced, and the tool brought to a halt when you reach the limit of the groove's travel. The end of the groove must then be cut square with the chisel and mallet.

As the groove does not run the full width of the wood, the board that fits into it will have to be notched at the end where the stop occurs.

The Shouldered Housing Joint

When the housing groove is cut so that its width is less than the thickness of the board that fits into it, the end of the board must have shoulders cut to reduce it to the required size. The shoulders are squared across both sides of the piece, and two parallel lines scribed along the end-grain with the mortise gauge, the distance between them being equal to the width of the groove. The shoulders can

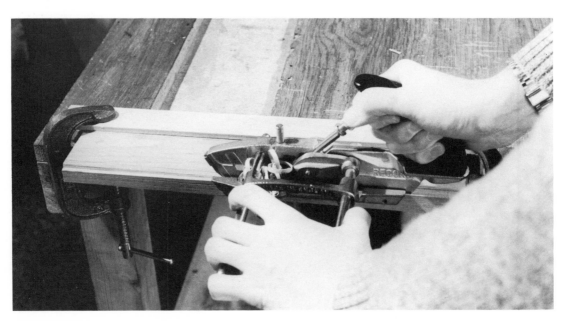

To cut the housing groove along the grain, the plough plane may be used.

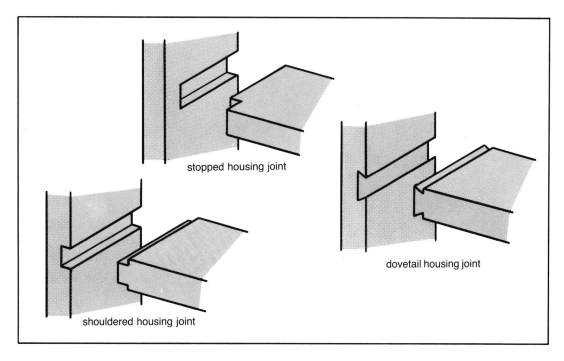

Three variations of housing joint: the stopped housing joint, shouldered housing joint and dovetail housing joint.

either be cut with the tenon saw, as when preparing a tenon, or the waste can be removed with the router fitted with a rebate cutter.

If the housing groove is stopped, a third and fourth shoulder will have to be cut to match the setting in of the groove.

The Dovetail Housing Joint

The dovetail housing joint is the most complicated type to prepare, and for this reason it is not very popular. It consists of a dovetailed groove, in which the sides are sawn at an angle so that the width of the groove increases with depth. In this case a third saw cut is needed. The first two form the sloped sides of the groove, and the third comes between the two to facilitate the removal of the waste, which should be cut out with a bevel chisel of approximately half the width of the groove, so that you avoid splitting any of the wood at the top of the dovetail.

Cutting a matching dovetailed tongue at the end of the board is a straightforward job of sawing two sloped lines along the end-grain, then making a cut on the shoulder lines to complete the removal of the waste. The two parts of the joint will probably need some trimming with the chisel before they slide to a perfect fit.

12 Halved or Lapped Joints

The halved joint, or lapped joint as it is also known, is used to join together two lengths of wood, usually at right-angles, by removing half the thickness from both pieces so that when they are brought into contact their surfaces remain flush. The joint can either be located along the length of the wood, or at the end of it. It may also be used to form oblique-angled joints, or for joining together the ends of two pieces in a straight line.

Mostly, the halved joint is applied to two pieces of wood when they are of equal thickness, but this need not necessarily be the case. In certain types occurring at the end of the wood, only the saw is employed for cutting, but with the other types, set along the length of the wood, the chisel is also used.

Provided it is measured accurately and cut with care, the halved joint offers a useful method of joining two pieces of wood with speed and simplicity.

TYPICAL APPLICATIONS

The halved joint has so many uses that it is difficult to point to any which could with justification be called typical. In fact, although it is so widely applicable, there are relatively few instances when it is employed in furniture-making. It is rather a contradictory sort of joint.

It can be used in a simple door frame construction, although this is not recommended for anything other than a small decorative door as you might find on a miniature cabinet. Its main use is in being able to provide a method of adding a rail or crosspiece to a structure after the main part of the frame has been built. Once fitted, it makes a good, strong durable joint.

METHODS OF PREPARATION

With most conventional halved joints, marking out and cutting the two halves is reversible – in other words, both parts are essentially the same. Strictly speaking, this is only true of the types that either form joints at the ends, or those that meet along the length of the wood. But even for a mixed joint, consisting of

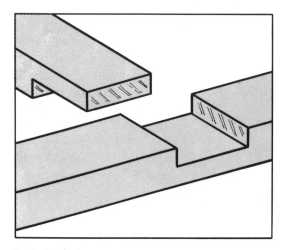

Exploded halved joint.

an end joined part of the way along the length, it does not matter where exactly the joint is placed. Once you have grasped the fundamental principle of its construction one halved joint is just like any other. This is also true for the oblique-angled variety, which differs only in respect of the angle at which one piece meets the other.

Joining at the Corner

This is the simplest type of halved joint, as it only involves the use of the tenon saw for cutting the wood. Let us assume that two pieces of wood, equal in width and thickness, are to be joined together at right-angles to form a corner, as in the construction of a door frame or some such similar item.

Begin by marking and cutting the end-grain of each piece square. Using the tape-measure, square and pencil, measure the exact width of the wood and set

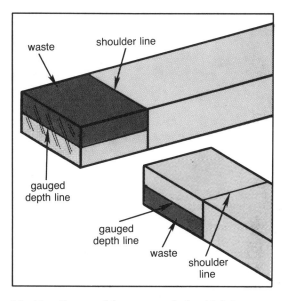

Marking the wood for a corner halved joint.

a line equal to this distance from the end-grain of both pieces, squaring the shoulder line across the side and repeating it on the two edges of the piece.

Set the spur of the marking gauge to exactly half the thickness of the wood. You can easily check to see if the tip of the spur is at that midway point by making a slight impression from both sides, and adjusting the fence slightly until the marks from the spur coincide.

Working from the face side of each piece, mark a line on the edges and end-grain in the area of the joint, scribing the edge lines up to the squared shoulder markings. To all intents and purposes, both the marked out portions appear identical, but by working the gauge from the same side in both cases, you have automatically corrected any slight error. Pencil a few criss-cross lines on the two waste portions.

To remove the waste, take each piece of wood in turn and clamp it in the vice. At first, it should be mounted at an angle of approximately 45 degrees. Place the blade of the tenon saw carefully against the marked lines – you should be able to see two quite clearly, the one on the edge nearer to you and the other on the end-grain – so that the kerf of the blade occurs completely on the waste side of the line. Hold the end of the wood firmly with your free hand, using your thumb joint to steady the saw blade.

Start the cut by making one or two firm strokes of the saw, and check that it is on the waste side of the lines. Carry on sawing until you reach the squared shoulder line that represents the depth of the cut. Take the piece out of the vice, turn it around and clamp it again so that this time the angle is reversed, and make the same saw-cut from the opposite side,

After sawing down the shoulder lines as far as the depth line, the waste is removed by clamping the piece upright in the vice and sawing down the end grain.

The completed joint, ready for assembly.

still keeping to the waste side of the line. Finally, place the piece upright in the vice, and complete the sawing down to the shoulder line.

Remove the wood from the vice and, laying it flat on the work-bench with its waste side facing uppermost, position the square so that it exactly coincides with the shoulder line drawn across the width of the wood. Score over it with the blade of a sharp knife. Place the piece on the bench hook and, holding it firmly, run the blade of a chisel across the grain on the waste side of the scored line, the chisel held at a slight angle so that its blade cuts a shallow groove. The purpose of this channel is to provide a slot in which the saw blade can run with accuracy to complete the cutting of the joint.

When both waste portions have been cut from the two joining pieces of wood, bring them together to check their accuracy. It may be necessary to trim off some waste with the chisel, manipulating it in a slow paring action until the two parts of the joint fit perfectly. The joint is assembled with wood glue, and the two halves held together with a G-clamp and small blocks of wood whilst the glue dries completely. For large halved joints, employed in the building of a heavy framework such as that of the carpenter's work-bench, it is advisable to strengthen them with woodscrews.

Joining End to End

The same type of halved joint can be measured and cut at the end of two pieces of wood so that instead of meeting at an angle of 90 degrees to form a right-angled corner, they continue in a straight line to increase the overall length of the assembled piece.

It would be rare to apply this method in furniture-making, because you can obtain the wood in long enough lengths without having to join them end to end. However, it does provide the cabinet-maker or restorer with a useful means of letting in a fresh piece of wood in place of a broken or woodworm-infested section on an existing item of furniture.

Preparation of an end-to-end halved joint is almost identical to that of a more conventional corner joint, except that in this case the length over which the joint runs is not limited to the width of the material but could, in theory, be any length you want. Practical considerations restrict its span, and it should be no more than twice the width of the material, perhaps less.

Joining along the Length

When the halved joint is to occur somewhere along the length of the two joining pieces of wood and not at the ends, the

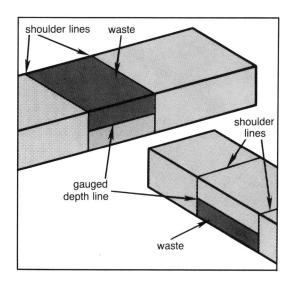

Marking the wood for a joint along its length.

method of preparation is somewhat different. Both parts of the joint still meet at right-angles, but instead of being open-ended, as in the previous examples, the two halves take the form of housing grooves cut in the sides.

Measure the pieces carefully to determine where along their lengths the joint is to be located. Having marked the position, square two parallel shoulder lines across the grain, separated by a distance equal to the width of the second piece, and continue marking around the two edges. To set the depth of the joint, adjust the spur of the marking gauge until it scores the wood half-way across its thickness. As long as both the pieces of wood are marked from the face side, it does not matter if the depth marking is slightly off-centre, as the two parts, when cut, must automatically add up to the overall thickness of the material.

Scribe the lines between the shoulder positions on both edges of the two pieces. Pencil a few criss-cross lines on the marked-out portions to serve as a reference so that you know at a glance which halves of the two marked areas are the waste. Removal of the waste is carried out in two stages, using the tenon saw, then the chisel. Taking each of the two pieces of wood in turn, place the square against the face edge so that the blade coincides with the position of the two squared shoulder lines, and score along each of them in turn with the sharp marking knife. Taking a chisel, work it across the grain just on the waste side of the two lines to pare off a sloped groove which acts as a guide for the tenon saw.

Hold the wood firmly in the bench hook, or clamp it at the edge of the workbench, and saw down to the half-way depth line at both ends of the marked-

111

The halved joint groove is cut by sawing a series of lines half-way down through the thickness of the wood and chiselling out the waste.

out area. In between, make a series of saw-cuts, parallel to the two already cut; the actual number will depend on the width of the joint but, to give you some idea, they should be spaced approximately ½in (13mm) apart from one another. All of these additional saw-cuts should be taken to within a fraction of an inch of the depth line.

With a ¾in (19mm) chisel, its blade honed to razor sharpness, remove the waste from between the two outermost saw-cuts. The best way of doing this is to work the chisel firstly from one edge and then from the other, tapping it gently with the mallet to dislodge the individual sections of waste, which will come away in small blocks. If you start by placing the chisel blade high up near the top of the wood, and gradually work it downwards

The completed joint, ready for assembly.

towards the depth line, you should avoid inadvertently chopping away too much at a time. Once you get near to the depth line, cease hitting the chisel with the mallet, but hold the tool horizontally and finish off with a paring action, removing thin slices as if you were planing the wood.

When the grooves are complete for both halves of the joint, bring the two pieces of wood together to test the fit of one half into the other. Assuming that all your measurements and markings were accurate, the shoulder of each groove should just make contact with the edges of the corresponding piece. If too little width has been cut away it will be loose. Preferably err on the small side, because at least you can trim the shoulders of the grooves to increase their width, whereas it is impossible to make a groove smaller once it has been cut.

To assemble the joint, mix some wood glue and apply it by brush to all the joining surfaces, bringing them together and holding under firm pressure with G-clamps while the glue sets. Screws can be used as an alternative to glue so that if desired, the joint can be dismantled again at some later time.

Joining at an Oblique Angle

So far, all the halved joints have formed corner or right-angled joints, or overlapped end-to-end in a straight line. There may be occasions, admittedly somewhat rarely, when you wish to assemble two pieces of wood at an angle of less than 90 degrees.

A halved joint formed at an oblique angle.

Regardless of whether this oblique-angled halved joint is to be at the end of the wood or along its length, the method of preparation is virtually the same as for the conventional right-angled joints already described – with one exception.

Instead of the right-angled square, an adjustable square is used, in which the blade can be altered to produce any acute angle. Once set to the angle required for the joint, this square is employed to mark all the shoulder lines across the sides of both pieces. The depth of the two halves is marked as before with the marking gauge, its spur set to a distance equal to half the thickness of the wood. Sawing and cutting methods remain unchanged.

13 Mortise and Tenon Joints

This is one of the most common and important joints in woodwork and furniture-making. It consists of a mortise, or opening, cut into one piece of wood, and a tenon, or tongue, equal in size to the mortise, cut in the second piece. It possesses great potential strength, can be adapted to a wide variety of uses, and in the majority of cases remains well concealed inside the wood. Its strength lies in the fact that the joining surfaces cover a relatively large area over which the wood glue can act.

There are a number of variations to this versatile joint. For example, some tenons are cut with two shoulders, while others are more refined with four. Those that have only one main shoulder are known as bare-faced tenons. Some mortises pass right through the wood to come out on the opposite side or edge, called 'through mortises'. Others stop short within the wood and are not visible from outside – 'stopped mortises'. There are also the haunched and mitred tenons.

For greatest strength, the assembled joints may be held firm with wedges or pegs. When pegs are fitted, the hole in the tenon is usually off-set slightly from the mortise hole so that the insertion of the peg pulls the joint tightly together, a process known as 'draw-boring'. Each of these main types will be detailed.

TYPICAL APPLICATIONS

The mortise and tenon joint occurs in such a variety of circumstances that it is virtually impossible to say that any one situation is typical. The joint lies at the very foundation of cabinet-making, and may be found in practically every aspect of work: the framing of chairs and tables, the building of cabinet carcases, the constructing of door frames.

Having said that, there are certain features which lend one particular type of mortise and tenon joint to one particular application, and this creates a number of divisions. Allowing for the inevitable overlap between these groups, it may be stated that table and chair building usually makes use of the four-shouldered stopped mortise and tenon; cabinet frameworks frequently use bare-faced, two-shouldered and four-shouldered stopped

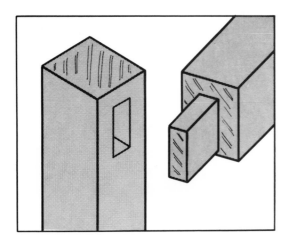

Exploded mortise and tenon joint.

mortise and tenons; cabinet doors are made with haunched or rebated mortise and tenons; larger doors generally employ through and wedged mortises, sometimes with double tenons; and the frameworks for heavy items, such as garden seats, are made from stopped, mitred and pegged mortise and tenons.

In deciding which type is best for any given piece of furniture, you must ask yourself the following: should the finished joint be visible or invisible; will it bear heavy loads and, if so, should it therefore be reinforced with wedges or pegs? With experience, you will find that the most appropriate type comes readily to mind, and there is often little doubt.

I have already mentioned that there is an increasing tendency for dowels to be used in place of mortise and tenon joints in the framing of tables, chairs and cabinets. This practice is to be discouraged, because the dowel joint has only a fraction of the strength possessed by an equivalent mortise and tenon joint. Where speed and simplicity are important factors, and the joint will not be subjected to heavy loading, the dowel joint offers a reasonable alternative. Even so, it can only imitate the layout of a four-shouldered stopped mortise and tenon joint; the remaining variations are impossible to copy or substitute.

PREPARATION

The Four-Shouldered Stopped Joint

As this is the most common type of mortise and tenon joint, we shall examine its preparation in detail. The many variants that follow from it will depend, to some

extent, on the techniques employed in this example. It is, as far as is practicable, a model mortise and tenon joint.

The theory of the mortise and tenon joint is that the mortise, and therefore the tenon, should be equal to one-third the thickness of the wood in which they are cut. This holds up perfectly when both parts of the joint are prepared from pieces of the same thickness, but it often so happens that the design of some particular item of furniture requires that one should be thicker than the other – the leg of a table or chair is of a greater thickness than the rail. It is usual to arrange for the mortise and tenon to be as large as possible, so that the one-third rule is applied to the larger thickness, which in most cases is that of the leg. Assuming that the rail is not less than one-third the leg thickness, a tenon can still be cut successfully, even though it has shallower shoulders.

However, for this example, I will assume that the mortise and tenon are to be cut from pieces of equal width and thickness. You first must check that the sides and edges are all planed straight and square. Even when the wood has been supplied by the local timber merchant to your own specified dimensions, it still pays to run the tape-measure over each individual piece to ensure that it is of the required width and thickness.

Start by marking in the position of the mortise. When it is to be set close to the end of the wood, as when forming a corner joint, you must allow at least 1in (25mm) extra to serve as a safety margin, so that as the mortise is being cut there is sufficient wood at both ends to prevent the piece from splitting. After the joint has been fitted together, this surplus is trimmed. There is no need to allow a

115

safety margin for a mortise placed along the length of the wood, because enough material exists at both ends of the joint.

Mark out with the tape-measure, square and pencil. Measure the distance from the end of the wood and square two lines across the edge of the piece where you want to make the mortise, separating the lines by an amount equal to the width of the rail in which the tenon will be cut. Continue squaring the lines around the wood.

Taking hold of the mortise gauge, set the distance between its two spurs to the width of the chisel that is nearest in size to one-third the thickness of the leg, and adjust the fence of the gauge until the two spurs make a pair of tiny impressions centrally on the edge. You can easily check whether or not the two points are dead-centre by holding the fence against each of the opposing sides in turn. When the pair of impressions coincide from both directions, you know that they are precisely in the middle. Having said that, it is still advisable to work the gauge from the face side for all marking operations.

Run the gauge along the edge of the wood so that the two spurs inscribe a pair of parallel lines between the two squared pencil lines. Hold the fence of the gauge firmly between forefinger and thumb, with the remaining fingers tucked around the shaft, and work the gauge in two or three even strokes to leave lines that are neither too faint nor too bold.

As the tenon is to have four shoulders, the next task is to measure and mark the setting in of the mortise at each end. These amounts depend on the length of the mortise and where it is situated. For example, when the mortise is positioned very near to the end of the wood, the distance by which it is set in is equal to the amount separating the shoulder of the tenon from the end-grain. The other

The distance between the spurs of the mortise gauge is set to equal the width of the chisel nearest in size to one-third the width of the wood in which the mortise is to be cut.

Marking out the mortise and the tenon.

end of the mortise needs only a small setting in, so that the tenon is not visible when the joint is assembled. When the mortise is placed along the length of the wood, far removed from either end-grain, it only need be set in by a small amount at both ends.

Decide how much of an inset you require, and measure this distance at the two ends of the mortise with the tape-measure, marking with the pencil and squaring across the edge of the piece. The mortise has now assumed the shape of a clearly-defined box, bounded by a pair of inscribed tramlines and squared pencil lines.

One further point must be considered before chopping out the mortise can begin, and that is how far down into the wood it should be cut. The generally accepted rule for a stopped mortise is that it should be equal in depth to three-quarters the width of the piece in which it is cut. This is admittedly a somewhat arbitrary figure, because there are often occasions when the wood is of quite a substantial width and you do not want to cut the mortise very far down.

The mortise should certainly never be cut any deeper than three-quarters of the way down, otherwise there is a danger of the wood splitting on the opposite edge. Decide on the depth of the mortise, then make a simple depth gauge by measuring off this distance on a piece of narrow dowelling and marking it in pencil so that it can be placed in the mortise from time to time as a check on progress.

Although it is perfectly feasible to remove all the waste from the mortise with the chisel and mallet, this is an unnecessarily long, drawn-out task. To speed up the process, much of the waste may be drilled out by boring a series of holes

along the length of the mortise. It is important that the drill bit should be slightly smaller in diameter than the width of the mortise, so that each drilled hole fits comfortably within the scribed tramlines, with room to spare. Having already determined the depth of the mortise, set a depth gauge on the drill bit. The simplest type is a piece of sticky tape wrapped around the stem of the bit.

Clamp the wood securely to the surface of the work-bench, or mount it firmly in the vice and, commencing from one end of the mortise, bore out a row of holes, each one set as closely as possible to the next. You can use the electric drill and vertical drill stand to carry out this part of the operation, though you will have greater control with the handbrace.

Taking the same chisel that was used to set the gap between the spurs of the mortise gauge, chop out the remainder of the waste. To begin with, make sure that the blade of the chisel is razor-sharp – its cutting ability can be tested by chopping into a piece of scrap wood to produce a clean cut down into the grain. Starting from the centre of the mortise, work outwards in both directions, striking the handle of the chisel hard with the mallet so that it cuts deeply into the wood. Every so often, unclamp the piece or remove it from the vice and turn it upside-down to clear out all the small scraps of waste.

The first chisel cuts are made with the chisel inclined at an angle so that, when worked from both directions, the cutting forms a V-shape. As you progress deeper and further back towards the two ends of the mortise, you should gradually bring the chisel up to the vertical. Stop a fraction of an inch short of the two squared end lines, because as you prise out waste

Waste is removed from the mortise by clamping the piece in the vice and drilling a series of holes along the marked area, using a drill bit slightly smaller in diameter than the width between the mortise tramlines. Set a depth guide on the drill bit equal to the required depth of the mortise.

When all the holes have been drilled, chop out the waste with the chisel and mallet.

from the deepest part of the mortise, you will find that the levering action of the chisel makes a dent in the wood. Once the mortise has been almost completely chopped out, you may then place the chisel blade on each of the two end lines and, with the tool held absolutely vertical, strike hard with the mallet to make a final downward cut to complete the mortise.

To mark and cut out the tenon, begin by taking the measurement for the depth of the mortise and transfer this distance to the end of the piece in which the tenon is to be prepared. Square right around the wood at this point, working the square from the face side and face edge. With the mortise gauge set as previously, scribe the two parallel lines along the two edges and the end-grain of the wood, working the gauge from the face side for all three pairs of lines.

Clamp the wood in the vice at an angle of approximately 45 degrees, and cut on the waste side of the marked lines with the tenon saw as far down as the squared shoulder line. Turn the piece around and repeat the same cut from the opposite

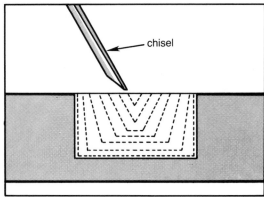

Pattern of chisel cuts for chopping out the mortise.

118

edge. Finally, holding it in an upright position, saw straight down.

Remove the piece from the vice and hold it flat on the work-bench. Place the square against each of the shoulder lines pencilled across the two sides of the wood, and score along both lines with the sharp marking knife. Cut a sloped channel on the waste side of the two lines, into which the blade of the tenon saw can be placed, and cut down to remove the shoulders.

The next job is to cut the third and fourth shoulders to match the setting in at both ends of the mortise exactly. Place the rail in position with respect to the leg, and make pencil marks on the tenon to indicate where the two ends of the mor-

The wood is clamped in the vice at an angle of 45° and the marked lines cut down with the tenon saw. Turn the piece around to repeat the same angled cut from the opposite edge.

The tenon is marked with the spurs of the mortise gauge set to the same gap as for the mortise.

Place the wood upright and saw down to the shoulder-line.

tise occur. Mark in these lines along the length of the tenon with the pencil and ruler. A special technique employed by experienced woodworkers is to grip the pencil so that the tips of your fingers press against the edge of the wood, and run your hand up and down the length of the tenon to make a straight line with the pencil's point.

Clamp the piece upright in the vice again and saw down the lines as far as the main shoulder line, then re-position it so that it lies horizontally in the vice, and complete cutting off the waste to create the second pair of shoulders.

In theory, the tenon should now fit snugly into the mortise with only light pressure applied to it. After all, both parts of the joint were marked to the same width and respectively cut on their waste sides. But you will usually discover that the cheeks of the tenon bind on the inside walls of the mortise, caus-

ing resistance which prevents the two parts from fitting fully together. The solution, of course, is to trim the tenon in the place where the binding occurs. This is easily located by removing the tenon from the mortise and examining its two main cheeks. You will notice that where the jamming is caused by one or other of the cheeks being too full, the trouble-some area has a shine to it, brought about by rubbing against the walls of the mortise. The same tendency to bind can also affect the two narrower cheeks, so these should be checked likewise.

To rectify the problem, place the rail flat on the work-bench and gently pare off a few slices of wood from the offend-ing part of the tenon, using the chisel held horizontally. Test the fitting of the joint again, trimming off more of the tenon where necessary. You will some-times find that a small chunk of wood has been left at the bottom of the mortise,

Chisel out a shallow groove along the shoulder-line to serve as a guide for the tenon saw.

Clamp the piece flat on the work-bench and saw down the shoulder-lines to remove the waste.

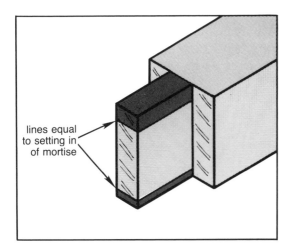

lines equal to setting in of mortise

Mark in the second pair of shoulders for the tenon.

The two parts of the joint are fitted together. If there is any tendency to bind, pare off thin slices of wood from the offending area with a wide-bladed chisel.

preventing the tenon from entering fully. This should be carefully chopped out. Eventually, the two parts of the joint will slide completely into place. Check the adjacent sides are flush with one another, and the joint does not wobble loosely.

The stopped mortise and tenon joint is assembled with wood glue, the glue being applied to all the joining surfaces with a brush, and the two parts tapped together and cramped securely for the duration of the glue's drying time.

The Two-Shouldered Through Joint

The main difference between this version of the mortise and tenon joint and that described in the preceding section is that the mortise passes right through the width of the wood, and the tenon has only two shoulders instead of four. It follows that this type of joint has greater potential strength since it acts over a larger surface area.

As far as the marking out of the mortise is concerned, the only difference between the through and the stopped mortise is that in this case the mortise must be marked on both edges in such a way that the two positions correspond exactly. The squared pencil lines that denote the length of the mortise are marked all around the wood, and the pair of tramlines scribed with the mortise gauge are scored on both edges, working the gauge from the same face side.

The cutting of the mortise is carried out from both edges, using the same method of drilling out the first stage of the waste and then chopping out the remainder with the chisel and mallet. However, this time each operation is performed to pass half-way down through the width of the

121

wood so that the cuts meet at the centre and thus form a hole that travels completely through the piece.

The tenon is cut in exactly the same manner as the four-shouldered tenon, except that its length is now matched to the width of the wood in which the mortise has been cut, and only one pair of shoulders is sawn off, leaving the width of the tenon equal to the width of the rail. In other words, there is no setting in for either the mortise or the tenon.

The trimming and fitting of a through mortise and tenon needs special care, because the end of the tenon is visible on the outer edge of the mortise piece. It should be mentioned that a through mortise can receive a four-shouldered tenon, in the same way that a stopped mortise can receive a two-shouldered tenon.

The Haunched Tenon

In certain types of door construction, a groove is cut centrally along the inside edge of the stiles and rails to receive a plywood panel which, when the frame has been assembled, is fixed permanently in position.

When it is possible to arrange for the tenon to be equal in thickness to the width of the groove, the mortise is merely cut as an extension to the depth of the groove in the required place.

The tenon is then cut with its third shoulder sawn deliberately short to leave a projection known as a haunch, which is equal in length to the depth of the groove and thus fits fully into it. As a result, once the door frame is assembled, it is virtually impossible to detect the presence of the groove along the top and bottom edges of the door.

The Mitred Tenon

This method is used when two rails are joined at right-angles to the same leg, so that the two stopped mortises combine with one another deep inside the wood. If each tenon were cut to fit its own mortise, a part of it would block the entry of the other – so the problem is resolved by cutting 45-degree mitre joints at the end of the both tenons, enabling each one to fit fully into its own mortise without interfering with the other.

There is no point in trying to arrange for the mitred surfaces to meet and touch inside the joint, since little additional strength will be gained in comparison with the overall effectiveness of the mortise and tenon joint.

The Wedged Joint

Wedges are only employed in the assembling of the mortise and tenon joint when it is felt that the strain imposed upon the joint is likely to be so great that the power of the wood glue will not be

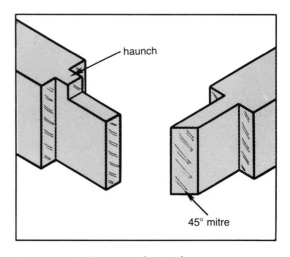

The haunched tenon and mitred tenon.

sufficient to hold its two parts together.

Two forms of wedging are possible. The first is used with a through mortise, where the outer part of the mortise is cut to a greater length than the inner, causing the two ends to diverge. Two slots are then sawn in the end of the tenon, and into each of these a hardwood wedge is driven, splaying out the two edges until the tenon fully occupies the mortise. The wedges are glued into their slots, making a permanent fixture in which it is impossible to pull the tenon out from the mortise.

The second type, known as the fox wedge, works on the same principle but is applied to the stopped mortise in which the end walls are cut at an angle so that the further down into the wood they go, the further apart they are set from each other. Once again, two thin slots are cut in the end-grain of the tenon and a thin hardwood wedge placed at the entrance of each one, so that as the tenon is driven down into the mortise, both the wedges are pushed completely into their slots, spreading the tenon fully into the mortise and locking it tightly in position.

The Pegged Joint

Pegging a mortise and tenon joint is favoured when the mortise is stopped and the wood is particularly hard. The peg has been in use since the earliest days of woodwork, long before screws and nails appeared. With the advent of powerful wood glues, the need for the peg has somewhat diminished, but it still retains one important function – and that is the process known as draw-boring.

In draw-boring, holes are bored through the sides of the mortise and tenon. This is done so that, with the hole in the tenon being slightly off-set from those in the mortise, when a dowel peg is driven in it serves to draw the tenon further into the joint. The result is a very secure fixture.

A small or medium-sized joint will only require one peg, but a large joint bringing together the components of a heavy seat frame, for example, will certainly need two. The dowels may be ¼in (6mm) or ⅜in (9mm) in diameter, and their receiver holes are drilled with matching bits.

The positioning of the hole, or holes, is not critical, but you should aim for it to be somewhere near the centre of the tenon cheek for a single peg, or spaced regularly apart for two pegs with plenty of tenon on either side. Once the posi-

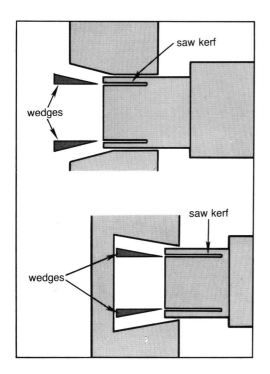

Two methods of wedging the mortise and tenon firmly together.

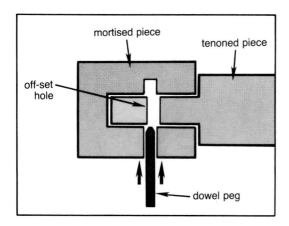

Draw-boring.

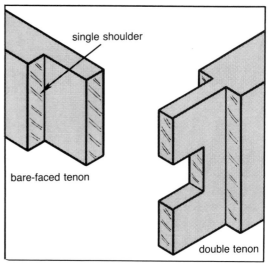

The bare-faced tenon and double tenon.

tions have been roughly determined on the cheek of the tenon, it is a simple matter to transfer these by measurement to the side of the mortise. Although the drilled hole must pass right through the mortise and into the wood on the other side, it must not be allowed to break through on the opposite side of the wood's thickness, so it is a stopped hole.

Cut the peg material to length and chamfer the end that is to be driven into the hole so that it has the ability to push its way into the off-set tenon without baulking, as would be the case if the end were left square. The pegged mortise and tenon joint is glued together but, due to the pulling effect of the draw-boring techniques, there is no need to cramp up the assembly.

The Bare-Faced Tenon

Unlike the conventional tenon, which has either two or four shoulders, the bare-faced tenon occupies one side of the wood and therefore has either one or three shoulders, depending on whether there is to be a setting in along its two edges. One cheek of the bare-faced tenon

lies flush with the side of the piece in which it is cut and, as there is only one scribed line running along the two edges and the end-grain (usually set about mid-way across the thickness of the piece), the marking can be carried out with the marking gauge instead of the mortise gauge. In all other respects, preparing the bare-faced tenon is the same as for an ordinary tenon.

The Double Tenon

If the tenon is to be cut in a particularly wide piece of material, such as the rail for a large door, the normal procedure is to cut it into two parts, so that it forms a double tenon. The mortise, likewise, is prepared in two sections, with a shallow groove bridging the gap in between. The reason for this arrangement is that the resulting joint is less susceptible to the effects of shrinkage within the wood. It is used mainly for household doors, and there is little call for it in the majority of furniture joints.

14   Bridle Joints

For the bridle joint two shoulders are cut away from one piece, at the point along its length where the joint is required, and a receiver slot cut in the other piece so that the two parts fit together at right-angles. The slot is equal in width to one-third the thickness of the wood. Marking is done in exactly the same way as for the mortise and tenon, but the areas that count as waste in the mortise and tenon are retained for the bridle joint, and vice versa. The bridle joint, when it is formed at the end of two pieces of wood, is often referred to as the slot mortise and tenon. It may be used in multiple form when joining together two boards, and is a useful alternative to the dovetail joint.

Exploded bridle joint.

TYPICAL APPLICATIONS

It would be impossible for the bridle joint to look as neat and unobtrusive as the stopped mortise and tenon joint, which takes precedence in all frame construction where rails are to be joined to legs, or some such arrangement. There is rarely any gain in cutting the bridle joint instead of the through mortise and tenon, because the latter can be wedged or pegged so easily.

The multiple bridle joint probably offers the greatest scope, because as a substitute for the dovetail joint it permits you to assemble two boards at right-angles, end to end, without having to measure all the dovetail angles so carefully. Of course, it is no outright replacement for the dovetail, because, without the sloped pins and sockets of the dovetail design, the bridle joint can be pulled apart from either direction.

METHODS OF PREPARATION

The Single Bridle Joint

As I have said, marking out the bridle joint is exactly the same as for marking the through mortise and tenon, provided it is of the two-shouldered variety. A bonus with the bridle joint is that when the joint is to form a corner with both

125

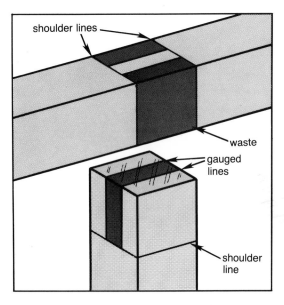

Marking out the bridle joint.

The completed joint, ready for assembling.

parts cut at the end of the wood, there is no need to add on extra material as a safety margin.

Cutting the shoulders from the one piece uses the same method as when preparing the halved joint, except that a shoulder is cut from each side. To prepare the slot in the second piece, make two saw-cuts down to the depth line with the tenon saw, working the blade on the waste side of each gauged line, and chop out the centre portion with the chisel, cutting from both edges to meet up half-way across the width of the piece. Trimming and fitting together the joint are the same as for the through mortise and tenon.

The Multiple Bridle Joint

When preparing a multiple joint arrangement to assemble two boards at right-angles, as in the building of a simple cabinet carcase construction, begin by taking the two boards, and mark and cut

the ends square. Measure the thickness of each board, which should be the same, and mark this distance from the end of the two pieces, squaring across the width in pencil and continuing the line right around both boards.

Assuming that the boards are of equal width – though they do not necessarily have to be – measure the exact distance from one edge to the other. This measurement must be divided into a number of segments. Exactly how many you have depends on the width of the boards and the chosen size of the slots and tongues that make up the bridle joint. Remember, though, that there should always be an odd number of segments, because on one board you start and finish with a slot, and on the other board you start and finish with a tongue, so that the joint forms an alternating pattern.

The easiest way of finding the most appropriate number of segments and the width of each one is to take the overall width of the board, either in inches or millimetres, and look for the odd number

126

that divides most conveniently into it. It does not matter if you have a fraction of an inch or a few millimetres left over, because this surplus can be divided in two and added to the two outermost segments for an even balance.

It is suggested that you make a card template, with the slots and tongues all marked out and cut to size with the sharp knife, and use this template to set the positions of the segments. Align it with the squared shoulder line marked across the width of each board, and pencil in a series of lines indicating the divisions between the segments. The point of the pencil must be very sharp to leave a thin line. Place the template against both sides of each board, and join up the lines on the end-grain. Wherever a slot occurs, mark this as a waste portion by making a series of criss-cross lines in pencil, and before you start cutting, make sure that you have set them in alternative positions between the two joining boards.

Taking each board in turn, clamp it upright in the vice and cut down on the waste side of each line with the tenon saw, working it down as far as the shoulder line. Where the slots are placed next to the edges of the board, saw down the shoulder line to remove the waste. The rest of the slots must be chopped out with the chisel and mallet, clamping the wood firmly at the side of the workbench. Chop firstly from one side, then turn the piece over and complete the cut from the opposite side, making a final trim of the shoulders with the chisel held vertically.

When all the slots have been cut, and the sides of the tongues trimmed to the waste lines, make a trial fitting of the two parts. If you have measured and cut accurately, the tongues should all fit perfectly into their slots. The joint is assembled with wood glue and cramped up for the period that it takes to dry completely.

A card template is used to mark out the slots for the multiple bridle joint.

The finished multiple bridle joint, ready for assembly.

15 Dovetail Joints

The dovetail joint ranks next to the mortise and tenon joint in importance, and yet many woodworkers are reluctant to use it because of its apparent complexity, as represented by the number of components and the angles at which they are cut. It is certainly true that the preparation of the dovetail joint requires considerable care and precise cutting, but this same principle applies to most other joints.

In its simplest form, the common dovetail joint consists of two parts. The first of these is the dovetail, which is a fan-shaped tongue cut at the end of the wood; and the second part is the angled socket into which the dovetail fits. The joint possesses great strength and has the ability to resist pulling apart in one direction owing to the wedge shape of the dovetail housed within its receiver slot, regardless of whether or not glue has been applied.

The joint is usually employed with a series of dovetails arranged in a row. The dovetail can either pass through the thickness of the piece to which it is joined, or it may be lapped, in which case it fits into a stopped receiver socket. A further variation is the mitred dovetail. Both the lapped and mitred dovetails are concealed from view once they have been assembled, and are therefore ideal in circumstances which dictate that the joint should not be seen. The dovetail joint is always assembled with glue. It is never screwed or nailed together.

TYPICAL APPLICATIONS

The most common application of the dovetail joint is in drawer construction, where two side panels need to be joined rigidly to a front and back panel. Indeed, the quality of a cabinet is often judged on the standard of finish evident in the drawer dovetails. This may seem a little unfair, but it indicates the importance generally attached to this joint. A drawer that is assembled with dowel joints is considered vastly more inferior, unless there is good reason for using this alternative method.

The dovetail joint can also be used to

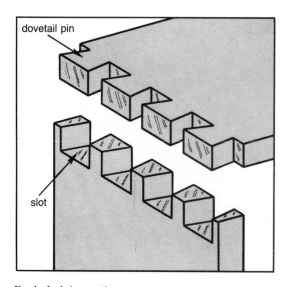

Exploded dovetail joint.

put together the carcase of a cabinet. However, it must be remembered that, unless you opt for lapped or mitred dovetails, the joint will be visible from two surfaces; this could prove a disadvantage. Used singly, the dovetail enables a rail to be joined to a framework, and its resistance to any tendency to pull apart makes it a perfect joint for large cabinet constructions where the weight of the structure places a strain on the individual parts.

METHOD OF PREPARATION

The Common Through Dovetail

It is best to begin with the simplest type of dovetail joint – the sort used in drawer construction. This forms the basis from which more advanced dovetail patterns are developed.

As the dovetail requires accurate angles, it is a good idea to start by cutting out a card template so that the correct angle can be maintained throughout. Angles do vary according to circumstances, but the dimensions of your template serve as a good guide. The first step is to mark and cut the ends of the two joining pieces perfectly square, planing where necessary. Measure the thickness of the material and set a shoulder line by this distance from the end of both pieces, squaring right around.

The number of dovetails per joint is determined mainly by the width of the wood, and the distance between each one. There is no rigid formula to stick to, but remember that the narrowest part of the dovetail must be sufficiently wide to

maintain its strength and prevent it from snapping off. It is convenient if the width at the narrowest part of each dovetail is equal to the width at the maximum part of the adjoining socket. For the two outermost dovetails, the distance between their narrowest parts and the adjacent edge of the wood should be half the above amount.

From this arrangement, you can work out a formula. Count the number of dovetails you want, double it to include the sockets, remembering that at each edge you have only a half-socket, and the sum of the dovetails and sockets gives you the total number of segments into which the width of the wood must be divided. If the proportions look wrong, try again with a different number of dovetails, until you are satisfied that you have reached the correct balance.

Mark out the segments along the shoulder lines with the tape-measure and pencil, starting and finishing in each case with a half-segment. Place the card template in position and mark in the slopes of the dovetails, joining them up on the end-grain. Clamp the piece upright in the vice, and saw on the waste side of the sloped lines with the tenon saw, cutting down to the shoulder line.

Chop out the waste between the dovetails with a bevel chisel and mallet. It helps if you make an extra saw cut in the middle of the waste portion. The bevel chisel is used because the bevels match the slopes of the dovetail sides. Work it to make a clean vertical cut along the shoulder line, chopping from both sides of the wood so that the cuts meet halfway through. Remove the narrow waste portions from the ends with the tenon saw.

Now clamp the second piece of wood

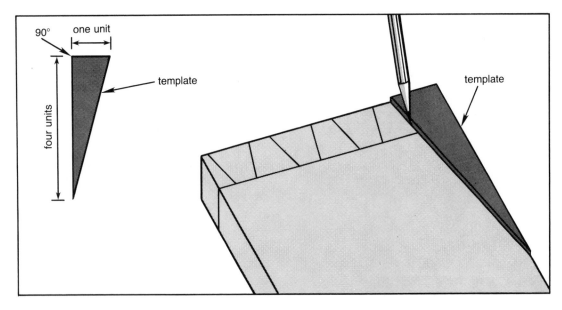

Marking out the dovetail joint. Recommended proportions of template are shown top left.

The wood is clamped securely upright in the vice and the dovetails cut down to the shoulder-line with the tenon saw.

Laying the wood flat on the work-bench, chisel out the waste from between the dovetail pins with a bevel chisel.

upright in the vice, and place the first piece with the finished dovetails against the end-grain so that the edges lie flush, and pencil in the slopes of the dovetails. With the square, mark the lines from the end-grain down to the shoulder line to define clearly where the sockets are to be cut. Saw down the sides of the sockets to the shoulder line, then hold the piece firmly on the top of the work-bench and chop out the waste with the chisel and mallet. The blade of the chisel must follow the direction of the sloped sides.

Unlike other joints, the dovetails must not be fitted experimentally into their sockets to check that both parts fit well, because this will place undue strain on the joint when it comes to separating them again. The most you can do is line them up and check visually for accuracy.

When the joint is ready for final assembly, apply wood glue to the joining surfaces, knock the two pieces together with the mallet and a block of scrap wood, and cramp up tightly until the glue has set hard.

The Lapped Dovetail

The principle of this joint is the same as for the previous example, but the main difference is that the length of the dovetail is less than the thickness of the wood in which the sockets are cut, so that in effect the sockets are stopped. The preparation of the dovetails remains the same, but greater care will be needed to cut sockets that stop short, and most of the waste will have to be removed with the chisel.

Place the dovetailed part of the joint accurately on the end grain of the second piece and carefully mark in the positions of the slots.

The finished joint, ready for assembly. It is not possible to make a test fitting of the dovetail joint without risking damage to the interlocking pins and slots. Instead, the two parts should be compared visually before attempting to glue them together.

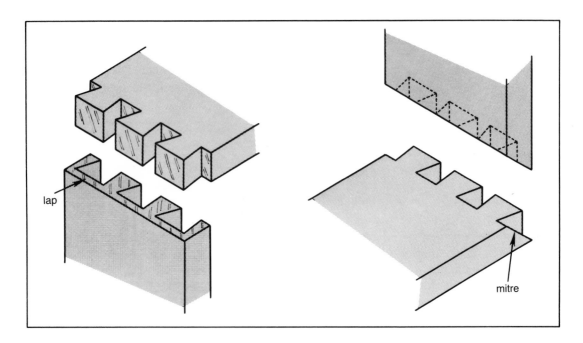

The lapped and mitred dovetail joints.

The Mitred Dovetail

Even more complicated than the lapped dovetail, the mitred dovetail calls for great skill if the two parts are to meet and join successfully. The method is broadly similar to the lapped variety, except that marking and cutting the dovetails and sockets must be combined with preparing the mitres at the end of each piece.

16 The Lyre-Legged Table

CUTTING LIST

Table top: one of 25¼ × 14¾ × ¾in (642 × 375 × 19mm)

Leg: two of 12¾ × 7 × ¾in (324 × 178 × 19mm)

Cross-rail: two of 11 × 1¼ × ¾in (280 × 32 × 19mm)

Foot: two of 11 × 1⅝ × 1¼in (280 × 42 × 32mm)

Stretcher rail: one of 21¾ × 2 × ¾in (552 × 50 × 19mm)

Peg: two of 2 × ⅝in (50 × 16mm) diameter

The finished lyre-legged table.

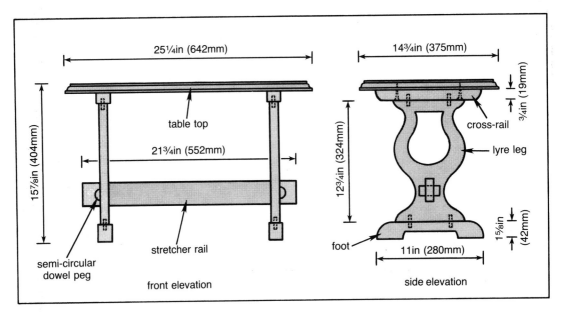

Front and side elevations.

CONSTRUCTION

This small reproduction-style occasional oak table has its origins in the design of the traditional refectory table. It has a rectangular top, two shaped legs mounted each on a foot, and a stretcher rail joining the legs near the bottom, passing right through to project slightly beyond. The legs themselves are cut in the form of a lyre, which is an old-fashioned string musical instrument that gave rise to the popular curved configuration towards the end of the eighteenth century.

Some original lyre examples went as far as to fill in the centre opening with metal rods to act as artificial strings, but in this table they are omitted for simplicity, since the plain rectangular top does not demand decoration to such an extent. The oak may be obtained from solid boards yielded by breaking up old ward-

robes or headboards. These must be lightly skimmed to remove all traces of the original surface finishes, revealing fresh layers. The boards should preferably measure ⅞in (22m) thick to start with, reducing to a thickness of ¾in (19mm) with the planing.

Having prepared the material satisfactorily, the next task is to make a template for the legs. This should be drawn on to a piece of thick card with a pencil, ruler and curved art stencil. When completed, cut it out using a sharp knife. Lay the template on the oak board, with the grain running from the top to the bottom of the leg and make two identical patterns, marking all around the template in pencil, including the opening. Clamp the wood securely to the side of the workbench and cut out the two legs using either the coping saw or the electric jigsaw fitted with a fine-toothed blade.

It requires careful manipulation to fol-

134

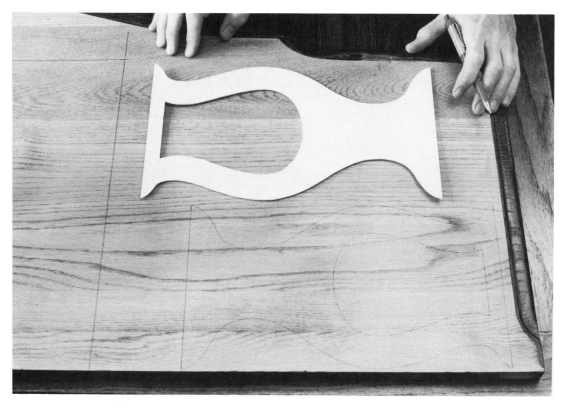

A card template is prepared to the required shape, and laid on the board of oak.
The outline of the lyre is then marked clearly in pencil.

low the curves. With the jigsaw in particular, which operates at high speed, there is a tendency for the blade to bind on tight corners, causing the body of the saw to vibrate and the wood to scorch. In this event, ease the saw back and work it forward again to complete the curve in short stages, always keeping to the waste side of the line. Any dark scorch marks will rub off with sandpaper.

The centre openings are cut in the same manner, but it is first necessary to bore out two holes, one at each top corner, just inside the marked out area. This provides access for the saw blade. If you are using a coping saw, you will have to slacken off the tension by unscrewing the handle. Slip the blade off its mounting notch at one end, and pass it through the one hole before re-assembling.

Drill out the two holes using a ½in (13mm)-diameter centre bit, boring down into the wood until the point of the bit just breaks through on the opposite side, then turn the piece over to complete the drilling. This simple method avoids splitting the surface of the wood. Once again, work the saw accurately around the bowl-shaped curve, and make a straight cut across the top, taking it fully into each corner.

Place the first leg in the vice, clamping it firmly, and smooth out any slight irregularities in all the curves with the spokeshave. At the same time, this will also remove any burnt wood on the tightest turns. Finish off by rubbing down with medium and then fine-grade sandpaper. Repeat the process for the second leg.

Measure and mark out the mortise positions on both sides of each leg. These are set to a length of 2in (50mm), equal to the width of the stretcher rail, and ½in (13mm) wide. Remove the bulk of the waste by making a series of holes inside the marked out area with a ⅜in (9mm) diameter centre bit, and chop out the mortise in each leg using a ½in (13mm) chisel, working it from both sides so that the cuts meet half-way through.

A piece of oak is fitted along the top and bottom end-grain of each leg. The one at the top acts as a cross-rail which attaches the leg to the underside of the table top, while the one at the bottom provides a foot for the leg to stand on. The cross-rail, cut from 1¼in × ¾in (32 × 19mm) material, measures 11in (280mm) in length, and is rounded off at each end. Use the art stencil to mark the curves. The foot is cut from 1⅝ × 1¼in (42 × 32mm) wood, also measuring 11in (280mm) long, and likewise has curves marked at each end. In addition, a portion is removed from the bottom edge to create the effect of two separate feet. Cut both pieces to shape with the coping saw or jigsaw.

The cross-rail and foot are attached to each of the two legs with dowel joints. Mark the dowel hole positions on the top and bottom end-grain of the legs, two dowels per joint, each one set in by 1½in (38mm) from the end, and placed centrally across the thickness of the wood. Clamping the leg upright in the vice, drill to a depth of ¾in (19mm) with a ¼in (6mm)-diameter centre bit mounted in

the handbrace. Check that each hole is drilled exactly perpendicular to the end-grain by placing the square against the bit.

The positions of the holes are now transferred by accurate measurement on to the bottom face of the cross-rail and the top edge of the foot, likewise being set midway across the thickness of each piece, and similarly drilled to a depth of ¾in (19mm).

Cut eight dowel pegs from ¼in (6mm) diameter dowelling, each measuring 1⅜in (35mm) in length. To facilitate the easy fitting of the dowels into their holes during assembly, chamfer the ends slightly by then giving one or two turns in a pencil-sharpener. Cut a single groove along their length with the hacksaw for the glue to squeeze out during assembly, thus reducing resistance to the fitting of each dowel.

Measure and mark the stretcher rail to length on a piece of 2 × ¾in (50 × 19mm) material. The tenon at either end projects 1½in (38mm) beyond the leg, and when this amount is added to the ¾in (19mm) thickness of the leg, it will be seen that each tenon will need to be 2¼in (57mm) long. Pencil in these positions and square around the rail.

Mark in the two tenons, setting the spurs of the mortise gauge to a gap of ½in (13mm) and adjusting the fence until they scribe a pair of lines centrally across the thickness of the rail. Score the lines along the upper and lower edges, and on the end-grain. Clamp the stretcher rail in the vice and cut off the waste with the tenon saw to create the two shoulders. Make a trial fitting of each tenon through its mortise to ensure that it slides easily without binding or jamming.

Mark in the position of the ⅝in (16mm)

diameter hole which is drilled through the tenons to take the semi-circular wooden fixing peg. The centre of the hole coincides with the outer face of the leg, ¾in (19mm) from the shoulder and positioned centrally across the width of the tenon. Make an identical marking on each of the tenon's two cheeks; then drill out the waste with a ⅝in (16mm)-diameter centre bit, working it from both sides so that the holes meet half-way through the wood.

Cut two 2in (50mm) lengths of ⅝in (16mm)-diameter dowelling and split each of these in half. Strictly speaking, one half should be slightly bigger than the other, so that its flat surface, which constitutes the diameter, can be trimmed smooth with the ⅝in (16mm) chisel. Fit the stretcher rail to the leg and slide the

peg into the semi-circular hole. If it does not quite enter the hole, trim a little more off the diametrical face of the peg.

The legs can now be experimentally fitted to the stretcher rail, with their two cross-rails and feet joined at top and bottom. It is important not to glue the joints just yet; but check to see that the feet stand square on a flat surface, and that the legs form right-angles with the stretcher rail.

Turning to the preparation of the table top, this is cut from a single oak board. Mark out its rectangular shape on the material, checking that all four corners are exactly square. Clamp the board firmly at the end of the work-bench, and saw off all the surrounding waste. Plane the edges to make sure they are perfectly flat and square.

Fitting together the dowel joint between the bottom of the leg and the foot. Before glue is applied to the dowels, the joint should be tested for accuracy.

The mortise and tenon joint between the leg and the end of the stretcher rail is assembled with glue and the semi-circular peg driven into place.

A decorative edge-moulding is given to all four edges of the table top using the electric router. A similar effect can be achieved with the plough plane. Either a corner round or Roman ogee profile can be given, depending on the type of cutter fitted to the tool.

The router is first worked along the two end-grain edges, as there is usually a tendency for the cutter to split the ends slightly. These are subsequently removed by working the tool along the grain. End-grain machining or planing is always harder work, and a tool like the router must never be forced along at speed, but allowed to progress slowly and evenly. Oak is a tough, hard, resist-

ing wood, and you are strongly advised to make at least three passes with the router, commencing with a shallow cut, then increasing the depth with the two subsequent passes. This will ensure that the wood offers less resistance, so the cutter will not overheat and scorch the edge. Rub down the fine strands of wood from the worked edges of the end-grain using medium-grade sandpaper, and finally smooth all four edge profiles.

Place the table top upside-down on the work-bench and lay the leg framework, also inverted, on its underside to mark in the positions of the two cross-rails. You will need to measure the distance between the cross-rails and the edges of the table to be certain that the legs are located centrally. Put small pencil reference marks at all four corners of each cross-rail to establish their final positions, then dismantle the arrangement.

Detach the cross-rails from the two legs, and mark two holes on the bottom side of each one, to take number 8 woodscrews. These holes will be used to attach the cross-rails to the underside of the table top, and they are set 6⅞in (175mm) apart so that eventually they will be concealed by the top of the leg.

Drill and countersink the holes. Fit a 1½in (38mm) number 8 woodscrew in all the holes – it does not matter whether they are brass or mild steel, since after assembly they are well out of sight and any staining will not be evident. However, mild steel is probably better, since it is less prone to shearing than brass.

Place the cross-rails back on the underside of the table top, following the pencil marks which should guide them to their precise positions, and give a few turns to each screw with the screwdriver so that their tips make an impression on the wood. Remove the cross-rails and drill down into the table top with the number 8 bit to a depth of ½in (13mm). Take care not to drill too far, otherwise you will risk breaking through the top surface.

Mix a small amount of wood glue, and apply it by brush to the upper side of the two cross-rails. Lay these in place, and screw them fully home. Make a final check that the remaining components have all been thoroughly rubbed down with fine-grade sandpaper. When you

are satisfied that they are perfectly smooth, apply glue to all the dowel joints and to the shoulders of the two tenons at the point when they mate with the mortise.

Assemble the feet to both legs, tapping the dowel joints fully together with the mallet. Do not strike too hard, or you will risk splitting the end-grain of each leg. Next, slot the tenon into its mortise at each end of the stretcher rail, joining it to the legs. Fit the dowel joints between the tops of the legs and the two cross-rails, knocking them tightly together. Apply a little glue to the semi-circular wooden pegs, and tap these into their receiver holes.

Wipe away excess glue from the surface of the wood with a damp rag, and cramp the assembly for at least a day whilst the glue sets hard. After the required period has elapsed, remove the cramps and give the table a further rub down with fine-grade sandpaper, paying special attention to the areas where the glue was wiped away, as it often leaves slight traces. Apply two coats of dark oak wood dye with a soft brush, working the stain quickly into the wood in smooth, even strokes. Allow the first application to dry thoroughly before applying the second.

Once the wood dye has dried completely, rub white French polish into the table, with up to four applications, covering all surfaces. The result is a rich shine which displays the oak grain perfectly. Thereafter, the table should be given a good wax polish every so often.

17 The Cheval Mirror

CUTTING LIST

Post: two of 42½ × 1⅞ × ⅞in (1,080 × 48 × 22mm)

Foot: four of 12 × 4¾ × ⅞in (305 × 121 × 22mm)

Top rail: one of 15⅜ × 2 × ¼in (390 × 50 × 6mm)

Bottom rail: one of 14½ × 3¾ × ⅞in (369 × 95 × 22m)

Mirror stile: two of 48½ × ⅞ × ⅞in (1,232 × 22 × 22mm) rebated

Mirror rail: two of 12½ × ⅞ × ⅞in (318 × 22 × 22mm) rebated

Back panel: one of 48 × 12 × ⁵⁄₃₂in (1,220 × 305 × 4mm)

Spacer block: two of ⅝ × 1⅛in (16 × 28mm) diameter

CONSTRUCTION

Named after the French word for horse, the cheval mirror dates back many years and consists of a long, narrow mirror held within a rectangular frame which is hinged between two vertical posts that form a stand. The mirror frame does not have to be perfectly rectangular, and some mirrors do indeed have ornamental arched shaping at the top. However, a straight edge all around makes for a simpler design which, when hinged exactly midway along its length, balances the mirror perfectly and allows it to remain in any chosen tilting position. A good quality hardwood such as sapele is used as a substitute for mahogany to make the mirror frame and the stand, its fine closely-textured grain being ideal for a piece of elegant bedroom furniture, with its potential for an excellent finish.

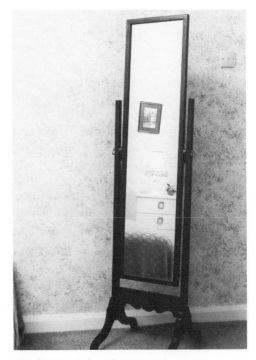

The finished cheval mirror.

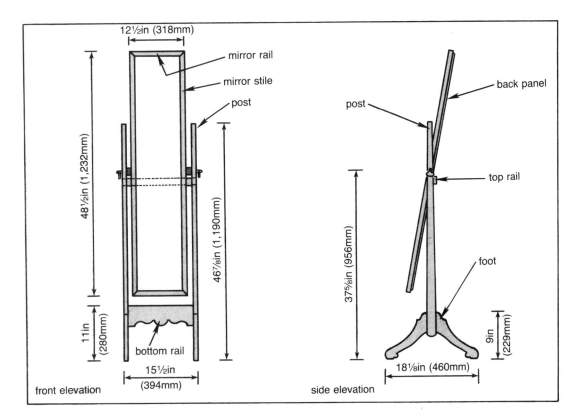

Front and side elevations.

Start by making the stand. This is a simple structure, comprising of two tapered upright posts, each of which has two symmetrical feet, joined by a shaped rail at the bottom and a thin plain rail higher up, just below the level of the hinge pivots.

The feet and bottom rail are assembled to the posts with mortise and tenon joints, whereas the top rail is merely butted up against the rear edge of the posts and screwed in place. Since all four feet are identical, it is best to draw out the required shape on a piece of stiff card to represent one foot, and cut out a template. Note that an extra ½in (13mm) must be allowed for the tenon. Lay the

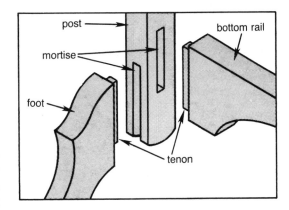

Exploded view of joints between feet, post and bottom rail.

141

template on a piece of sapele and mark out four identical feet, overlapping the curved portions as far as possible to make the most economical use of the wood.

Clamp the material securely to the side of the work-bench and cut around the four feet using the coping saw or jigsaw fitted with a fine-toothed blade. Work the saw carefully on the waste side of the lines, easing the blade around the tightest curves. In the case of the jigsaw, as with all high-speed cutting, there is a danger of the blade heating up on the turns due to friction between the sides of the blade and the wood. Some woods scorch very easily, and give off a lot of acrid-smelling smoke. Do not be alarmed when this happens, but draw the saw back a little to reduce the friction and

work it around the troublesome curve in short bites, keeping the blade operating at right-angles to the wood at all times.

When the four feet have been cut to size, line them up alongside each other to check that they are all the same; where minor differences occur in their contours, mark any unwanted projections in pencil, place the offending piece in the vice and trim away the excess with the spokeshave, finishing with sandpaper. Next, take two lengths of sapele for the vertical posts. At the bottom of each one a pair of feet will be attached, using a modified mortise and tenon joint. The modification is of the mortise, which is cut in the form of a single housing groove.

The mortises are marked in the following way. Firstly, for decoration, round

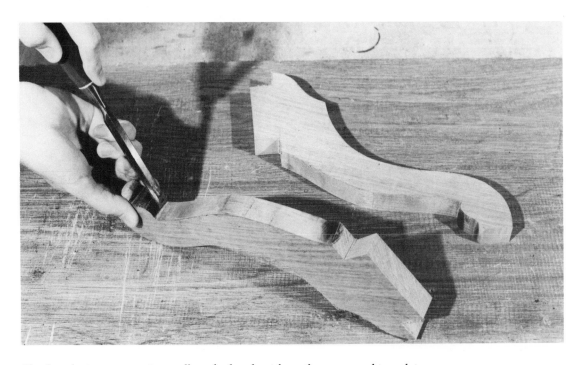

The four foot-components are all marked and cut from the same card template, and carefully trimmed with the spokeshave and chisel.

off the bottom end-grain of each post by marking in an arc of a circle with a pair of geometrical compasses. Remove the waste with the coping saw or jigsaw.

Now measure the length of the straight jointing end-grain of the foot – it should obviously be the same for each one – and mark this distance on the bottom edges of the post, taking the measurement from the curve. Square all around the post. Set the spurs of the mortise gauge to a gap of ⅜in (9mm), and adjust the fence until the lines are inscribed centrally along the ⅞in (22mm)-thick edge of the post. Set the mortises ⅜in (9mm) down from the line that denotes the upper limit of the foot.

Since the mortise runs out at the bottom end of the post, there are two methods available for its preparation. You can either use the traditional technique of employing the chisel and mallet, chopping the waste out bit by bit to a depth of ½in (13mm), or you can place a ⅜in (9mm)-diameter cutter in the electric router, and set it to cut out a housing groove inside the marked mortise lines to the same ½in (13mm) depth. Clearly, the spinning action of the cutter means that the groove will have a semi-circular end at the position near the top of the mortise where the router is stopped. Square off the end with the ⅜in (9mm) chisel.

Mark in the corresponding tenon along the straight end-grain of each foot, sawing off the waste with the tenon saw. When the two main shoulders have been prepared, set in a third shoulder ⅜in (9mm) from the top of the foot to match the setting down of the mortise. Make a test fitting of the joints, trimming where necessary to achieve a perfect fit.

The two vertical posts are gradually tapered to make the stand appear more graceful, commencing from a point beside the upper edge of the bottom rail. The object of the exercise is to arrange for the top end-grain of the posts to be square in cross-section. Since the material measures 1⅞ × ⅞in (48 × 22mm) to begin with, each taper will need to be taken down to a maximum depth of ½in (13mm). Mark in the two converging lines with a length of straight-edge and a pencil, then clamp the post horizontally to the work-bench and plane off the waste. When both tapers are completed for each of the two posts, mark in the position of the hinge pivots for the mirror frame, and drill through with a ¼in (6mm)-diameter centre bit, taking care to keep the handbrace perpendicular to the post.

The bottom rail is located slightly above the level of the two feet, for no other reason than that it breaks up the monotony of having three adjacent assemblies all at the same height. The placing of the rail is largely a matter of personal preference, as none of the three joints in each post interferes with the other two. What you must avoid, though, is positioning the bottom rail so high that it gets in the way of the mirror.

Having chosen its position, mark in the mortises as previously, keeping the gap between the spurs of the mortise gauge to the same ⅜in (9mm), but adjusting the fence to take account of the width of the material. Square in the desired position of the rail with the pencil and square, and set in the mortise by ⅜in (9mm) top and bottom. This is a true mortise, unlike the housing groove cut for the foot joints, so the standard method should be used in its preparation, drilling out some of the waste with a ¼in (6mm) diameter centre bit, and chopping out the remainder with the ⅜in (9mm) chisel and mallet.

For the bottom rail, it is wise to draw a template so that you can be assured of the symmetry of the curves along the bottom edge. Cut out the template as before, marking the outline in pencil on to a piece of sapele and adding an extra ⅜in (9mm) at each end for the tenons. Cut the rail to size using the jigsaw, trimming where necessary with the spokeshave, and rubbing down throughly with sandpaper. Mark the tenons to match the mortises and cut them to size.

Loosely attach the feet and bottom rail to the two posts, and measure for the top rail, setting its position ¼in (6mm) below the level of the hinge pivot holes. The top rail need only be 2in (50mm) wide and ¼in (6mm) thick, and you ought to be able to prepare it from some off-cut scraps of wood. Chamfer the top and bottom edges for neatness, and drill two number 6 countersunk screw holes at each end, one above the other. Place the rail in position, butting up against the rear edge of the two posts, and mark through the screw holes with the bradawl. Dismantle the assembly and drill holes in the two posts to a depth of ¼in (6mm).

Prepare some wood glue, and begin assembling the stand by joining the two feet to each post. Lay the two assemblies on a flat surface with the joints cramped tightly together while the glue dries and sets hard. Once this stage is completed, remove the cramps, and sandpaper the surfaces thoroughly.

Mix more glue and assemble the bottom rail to the two posts, cramping up firmly. Glue the butt joints between the top rail and the posts, screwing them together with four ½in (13mm) number 6

The top rail is butt-jointed to the rear edge of the two posts, and secured with glue and screws.

woodscrews. Allow plenty of time for the second stage of gluing to harden completely. When the cramps are taken off, fill any small gaps in the joints with mahogany-colour wood stopper, and rub down with fine-grade sandpaper.

The next step is to make the frame for the mirror. The stiles and rails are prepared from ⅞ × ⅞in (22 × 22mm) sapele, rebated along one edge to a depth of ⅝in (16mm) and a thickness of ¼in (6mm) to receive the mirror. The four corner joints are a combination of the bridle joint and mitre joint, with the mitre on the front face of the frame for visual appeal, and the bridle joint mostly hidden from view, behind, giving the frame its main strength.

As far as the rebating of the wood is concerned, you can either prepare your own rebates or ask the timber merchant to carry out the work for you. It is always more satisfying to do it yourself, by hand with the plough plane or with a power tool such as the router – but if you want

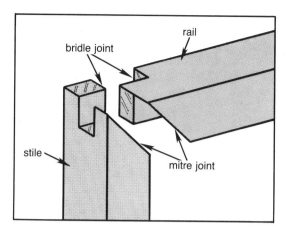

Exploded view of compound joint between the mirror frame rail and stile.

to save yourself the trouble, most wood yards will do the machining for only a little extra cost.

The first task when cutting the joints is to mark in the overall lengths of the stiles and rails, which are equal to the height and width of the frame respectively. Now the end of each piece must have its thickness divided into three segments – ¼in (6mm) for the forwardmost part, and ⁵⁄₁₆in (8mm) for the middle and rear parts. As you mark these in with the mortise gauge, it will become apparent that the ¼in (6mm) portion relates to the thickness of the frame material from its front surface back to the rebate, with the remaining two ⁵⁄₁₆in (8mm) portions dividing the depth of the rebate in half. The mitres occupy the front ¼in (6mm), and the bridle joint is cut to coincide with the other two.

Mark in the mitres with the mitre square, cutting off the waste with the hacksaw. Next, mark in the two parts for the bridle joint, consisting of alternating tongues and slots. The measurement and cutting of these must be very precise: for instance, a tongue at the end of the rail will fit into the slot cut in the stile.

Arrange for the depths of the tongues and slots to fall in line with the rebating. Remove the waste with the hacksaw and chisel. Trimming the joints where necessary, fit them together experimentally and check that they each form a perfect right-angle.

Mix a small quantity of wood glue, apply it to the joints with a small brush and assemble the framework, cramping it up on a flat surface. When the glue has set hard, remove the cramps and rub down thoroughly with medium-grade sandpaper, giving a rounded profile to the front face of the frame. Finish the rubbing down with fine-grade paper. Mark in the corresponding hinge pivot holes midway along the length of both stiles, setting them ⅜in (9mm) from the rear edge, and drill a hole through with the ¼in (6mm) diameter centre bit.

Apply a mahogany wood stain to the stand and the mirror frame with a fine brush, working the stain into the rebate of the frame. When this has dried completely, give several applications of French polish until the surfaces of the wood assume a rich shine. Purchase a sheet of ⁵⁄₃₂in (4mm)-thick mirror glass to fit into the rebated frame. The mirror size must be measured carefully from the distances between the rebates so that it drops in with ⅛in (3mm) to spare on each edge. Cut twelve small hardwood wedges from off-cut material, each measuring ½in (13mm) in length, and glue these to the inside of the rebates, tapping the sloped face of the wedge down against the glass. There should be two wedges to each rail, and four to each stile. Cut a panel of ⁵⁄₃₂in (4mm)-thick plywood to fit neatly at the back of the frame. Stain the outer surface with mahogany stain, and fix it to the frame with panel pins.

It only remains to hinge the mirror frame to the stand. You can buy small ornamental brass dropper handles which have a threaded tapping to receive a fixing bolt. In this instance, you will need to purchase a length of matching threaded bolt from an ironmonger's shop and cut two pieces with the hacksaw which are long enough to pass through the post and the mirror frame in addition to bridging the gap in between. Each gap is filled with a 1⅛in (28mm)-diameter piece of dowelling, cut to a length of ⅝in (16mm), both of which have a ¼in (6mm)-diameter hole drilled through their centres and, like the rest of the woodwork, are stained mahogany and French polished.

To fix the hinge bolt in place, slightly enlarge the hole on the outside surfaces of the mirror's stiles to house a hexagonal nut, and hold this securely by fitting a recessed rectangular brass plate over it, fastened with a small brass screw at each end, and with a hole drilled through its centre to admit the bolt. Screw the bolt tightly to the dropper handle then, hold-

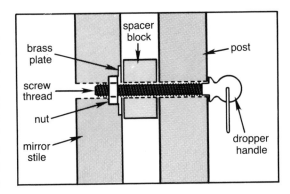

Hinge pivot detail.

ing the mirror frame and spacers in position, pass the two lengths of bolt through the holes and turn in a clockwise direction until they engage with their nuts. The dropper handles should not need to be fully tightened in order to hold the mirror in a tilting position, as it will remain at any chosen angle due to an equal distribution of weight at either end. Give the wood an occasional rub over with a good-quality wax furniture polish to keep the mirror and its stand looking at their best.

18 The Display Cabinet

CUTTING LIST

Side: two of 21½ × 3¾ × ¾in (546 × 95 × 19mm)

Top panel: one of 15⅛ × 4½ × ¾in (384 × 114 × 19mm)

Bottom panel: one of 14⅛ × 3¾ × ¾in (358 × 95 × 19m)

Pediment: one of 15½ × 3¾ × ¾in (394 × 95 × 19mm)

Frieze: one of 14⅛ × 2⅞ × ¾in (358 × 73 × 19mm)

Long cornice moulding: one of 15⅞ × ¾ × ⅜in (403 × 19 × 9mm)

Short cornice moulding: two of 4⅞ × ¾ × ⅜in (123 × 19 × 9mm)

Back panel: one of 18 × 14¼ × ½in (457 × 362 × 13mm)

CONSTRUCTION

All collections need a display cabinet if they are to be properly exhibited. This small wall-mounted cabinet is designed to hold miniature cars, china thimbles, glass figurines, or the many other items that form the basis of a personal collection. The main features of this cabinet are an open interior, three clear glass shelves for easy viewing, a velvet lining to the back panel, and an elaborately ornamented pediment set above the top panel, with a simpler curved frieze beneath the bottom panel.

The construction of the cabinet is quite straightforward. The top panel is joined to the sides with a version of the bridle joint, which employs multiple slots and tongues. The bottom panel is mounted to the sides with a single housing joint at each end, with the back panel and frieze attached likewise. The pediment is fitted

The finished display cabinet.

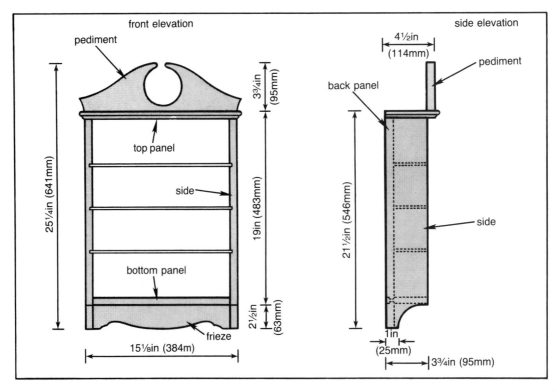

Front and side elevations.

to the upper surface of the top panel with dowel joints, and a decorative cornice moulding fixed to the front and two sides of the top panel, mitred at both corners. Apart from its aesthetic value, the cornice moulding is intended to conceal the otherwise exposed bridle joints.

The choice of material is obviously a crucial factor if the cabinet is to possess an air of elegance and distinction, so I would recommend you to select from the fine-grained and well-figured hardwoods such as teak, afrormosia, mahogany or sapele. There are, as always, various alternatives and you might prefer to make the cabinet in rosewood or walnut. The example opposite is made from sapele – indeed, due to the small size of the cabinet and the fact that the back

panel is cut from plywood, all the wood was obtained from off-cuts found lying around the workshop!

The initial step is to measure and mark out the two side panels, which are prepared from 3¾ × ¾in (95 × 19mm) material. At the bottom end, immediately beneath the level occupied by the bottom panel, a curved portion is marked in with a pair of geometrical compasses set to a radius of 2½in (63mm). Each portion is cut out with the coping saw or electric jigsaw and, if necessary, planed smooth with the spokeshave.

The bottom panel is cut to the same width as the sides, and its length measured to take account of the housing joint tongues that fit into grooves cut in the side panels. In the case of the top panel,

148

however, an additional ¾in (19mm) is given to the width so that the front edge overhangs the sides, and the length is the same as the overall width of the cabinet, due to the interlocking nature of the bridle joints.

The procedure for marking out the bridle joints is not difficult, but it must be carried out accurately if the slots and tongues are to engage correctly. The width of the two sides, being 3¾in (95mm) divides very conveniently into five segments of ¾in (19mm) each. The sixth segment is provided by the extra ¾in (19mm) of the top panel, which projects at the front. Carefully draw a pattern on to a piece of thick card to represent these divisions, marked to a depth of ¾in (19mm) (which is equal to the thickness of the top and side panels), and cut out alternate segments with a sharp knife. This gives you the basic pattern.

Placing this card template in position at the upper end of each side panel, and both ends of the top panel, mark in the segments on the wood with either the blade of the knife or the point of a sharp pencil. These lines must be as thin as possible, and yet clearly discernible. Square in a line ¾in (19mm) from the end to indicate the depth to which the seg-

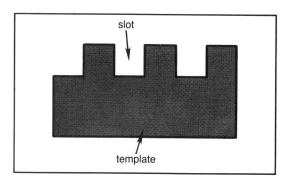

Template detail for bridle joints.

ments must be cut. You will see that there is only one possible way for the slots and tongues to be arranged, and that is by commencing from the projection at the front of the top panel and taking this to be equal to the full length of the piece. This, therefore, forms a tongue, and the next segment back is a slot, and so on. For the two sides, the tongues and slots occupy alternate positions.

The method for cutting out the slots is very similar to that employed when making a dovetail joint. Taking the two sides and top panel in turn, clamp the piece upright in the vice and saw down the marked lines with the tenon saw, always working its blade just on the waste side of the lines, and cutting down as far as the squared depth line.

Remove the piece from the vice and clamp it flat to the work-bench. Taking a ¾in (19mm) chisel and mallet, chop out the waste from between the saw-cuts. It is a wise precaution before commencing this operation to place both parts of each joint up against each other and mark the portions that are to be removed by pencilling a few lines criss-cross fashion on all the waste pieces. The blade of the chisel must be honed to razor-sharpness so that when the tool is held vertically on the depth line and struck hard with the mallet, the waste cuts cleanly away.

When all the slots have been successfully chopped out, make a trial fitting of the joints. If the slots and tongues do not immediately engage properly, trim the sides of the offending tongues with the chisel, paring off thin slices, a little at a time, until the two parts fit fully and easily together.

Once both sides can be assembled to the top panel, dismantle the bridle joints and mark in the position of the housing grooves for the bottom panel on the inside faces of the sides, using the square, pencil and tape-measure. The grooves are marked to a width of ⅜in (9mm), arranged to coincide with the midpoint of the shelf's thickness, and set in by ¼in (6mm) from the front and rear edge. At the same time, set the spurs of the mortise gauge to a gap of ⅜in (9mm), centralise them on the end-grain of the bottom panel, and mark in the tongue at each end. Note that the groove and tongue are cut to a depth of ¼in (6mm).

Prepare the groove in each side panel using the high-speed electric router fitted with a suitable cutter. Clamp a length of straight-edged batten across the width of the piece to act as a guide, and work the router carefully between the marked limits. Due to the circular action of the cutter, the groove will terminate at each end in a semi-circle. Square off the ends with a ⅜in (9mm) chisel. Place the bottom shelf in the vice and cut away the shoulders of the tongue with the tenon saw. Set in the tongue by ¼in (6mm) to match the groove.

It should now be possible to make a temporary assembly of the sides to the top panel and bottom panel, thus forming a box-type structure. When you are satisfied that the joints are all fitting fully and accurately, measure for the bottom panel, to include a tongue at each end which will be used to join it to the sides.

For the moment, however, concentrate on marking out the curved bottom edge, using an artist's stencil known as a French curve. The lowest point at either end must coincide with the bottom of each side. In reality, it can be rather difficult to achieve a perfectly flush fit between the two, since an additional ¼in (6mm) must be allowed at the top edge of the frieze which will be let into a groove cut along the underside of the bottom shelf. A certain amount of trimming will be called for after the final assembly. Carefully cut around the curved pencil marks on the bottom frieze with the coping saw or jigsaw, smoothing out any slight irregularities with the spokeshave and finally sandpapering the edge.

Using a similar technique, mark out the curves for the top pediment, drawing in the circle at the centre with the pair of compasses, and cutting out the pattern. The pediment is mounted on the upper surface of the top panel so that it lies flush with the front edge. It is attached with dowel joints. Five dowels are sufficient, arranged at regular intervals. Their positions should be measured along a line scribed on the upper surface of the top panel, and on the lower edge of the top pediment. The spur of the gauge should be set to a distance equal to

The housing grooves for the glass shelves are cut across the width of the two side panels between the front edge and the groove for the back panel, using the router.

half the thickness of the pediment so that the two lines, thus inscribed, coincide when the pediment is mounted in position.

It is now a simple matter to measure from the centre outwards, starting with the dowel that is placed midway along the joint, and marking the four remaining dowel locations at set distances. Repeat these positions for the second part of the joint, then drill out the holes with a ¼in (6mm)-diameter centre bit to a depth of approximately ⅜in (9mm) in the top panel and ½in (13mm) in the pediment. Cut five pieces of ¼in (6mm)-diameter dowelling each to a length of ¾in (19mm), chamfering the ends in a pencil sharpener. Place these to one side until you are ready to commence assembling the cabinet.

The next task is to cut the housing grooves for the back panel and the bottom frieze in both side panels. These grooves are marked to a width of ⅜in (9mm) and set in by ³⁄₁₆in (5mm) from the rear edge of the two sides. Clamp each side in turn to the end of the workbench, and cut out the grooves with the plough plane or router, setting it to a depth of ¼in (6mm). Each groove runs in a continuous straight line along the entire length of the side, cutting through the groove which has already been prepared to receive the bottom panel. The fact that a small rectangular hole will show at the top of the cabinet does not matter, as it will be out of sight.

Similarly, grooves are cut in the underside of the top panel, and the upper and lower sides of the bottom panel, to receive the back panel and frieze respectively. Mark a corresponding tongue on the upper edge of the frieze to fit into its groove. Make a further trial assembly of the cabinet, consisting of the two sides, the top panel, bottom panel and frieze. The presence of the frieze should now ensure that the structure has properly right-angled corners.

Measure for the back panel, noting that there will be two sets of dimensions: the length and width taken within the inside faces of the sides, top and bottom panels; and the slightly larger length and width measured to the depth of the four housing grooves. Cut a piece of ½in (13mm)-thick plywood to match the larger set of measurements, and prepare a rebate on all four edges so that the distances between the opposing edges is equal to the smaller pair of dimensions. Cut out the plywood with the jigsaw, and prepare the rebates with the router. Dismantle the cabinet, and insert the back panel to check that it fits well.

Decide on the height you want for each of the three glass display shelves. A regular spacing is advised. As the glass will be of 4mm thickness, the grooves that are cut to receive the shelves should be ¼in (6mm) wide, and ¼in (6mm) deep. Mark in the grooves with a tape-measure, square and pencil, and cut them with the router, working each channel from the front edge backwards to the groove that has already been cut for the back panel.

The cabinet is now ready for final assembly. However, before the glue is applied to the joints it is a good idea to give each component a thorough rubbing down with medium and then fine-grade sandpaper to remove all traces of pencil reference marks, and to produce a smooth surface. It is especially important to rub the curved edges well so that they flow gracefully.

Mix a quantity of wood glue and, applying it with a small brush, work it well into the joints between the one side panel, the bottom panel and the frieze. Bring all three parts together, and tap the joints home with the mallet. Now brush the glue into the remaining grooves on the two side panels, along the four re-bates on the edges of the back panel, and finally on to the tongues and slots of the two bridle joints. Knock the cabinet into shape, using a block of clean scrap wood to absorb the blows from the mallet. You may find that the back panel, which often tends to flex a little, needs gentle pressure to straighten it out so that it seats fully in its grooves. Cramp the cabinet tightly together, bringing pressure to bear between the two sides, until surplus glue squeezes out from the joints. Wipe this away with a damp rag, and leave the assembly for a day while the glue fully hardens.

When the cramps come off, mix some more wood glue and apply it to the five

The bottom panel and frieze are assembled to the sides with shouldered housing joints.

dowel joints attaching the pediment to the upper side of the top panel. Glue should also be brushed along the two joining surfaces, and to the dowels themselves. Tap the pediment down into place, and hold it with two small G-clamps, one at each end.

The front edge of the top panel is still exposed, together with the two bridle joints which are plainly visible at the top of the two sides. These must now be covered. The most appropriate material is a decorative piece of moulding with a classical profile, prepared from a hardwood which closely resembles that used for building the cabinet. This can pose quite a problem if you search the supplies of edge-moulding stocked by many DIY stores, since there is a distinct lack of imagination in many of the profiles, and the choice of material is often restricted to light-coloured ramin, or the coarser grains of some darker species of timber.

This is where a little ingenuity comes in useful. To begin with, you could cut your own mouldings, from sapele, using a combination of cutters with the plough plane or router. However, mention has already been made of the fact that old furniture can be picked up very reasonably second-hand, and certain items will often yield long strips of edge-moulding which can be carefully prised off and used again. It was from my own stock of recovered mouldings, rescued from some dismantled cupboard or headboard long ago and stored ever since, that I found a profile which seemed just right for the cabinet I made. Admittedly, it was made from oak, but at least the difference was not very obvious. The strip simply needed trimming along its lower edge to bring it to the correct ¾in (19mm) width.

Cut three pieces, one long length to

run across the width of the cornice, and two shorter pieces for the sides, and prepare mitre joints for each corner. Mix a small amount of wood glue, brush it on to the rear surface of the three lengths, and place them in position. Tiny veneer pins may be tapped through to make for a stronger fixture, but be careful not to split the wood in doing so. When the glue has dried, rub down the moulding to remove all traces of old varnish, or whatever was originally put on it.

The cabinet is now ready to be stained. Since the wood used in its construction is sapele, the most appropriate colour of stain is mahogany. Pour some of the liquid into a shallow vessel such as the lid of an old jam-jar, and apply the stain to the surfaces of the cabinet with a soft-bristled brush. There is no need to cover the inside face of the back panel (except at the edges) or indeed any of the cabinet's rear surfaces. When the stain has dried, give the surfaces several coats of French polish, or rub thoroughly with wax polish.

The cabinet interior is lined on its back surface with red velvet. Firstly, a piece of thick card must be cut to serve as a backing to which the velvet can be stuck. Measure exactly the internal dimensions, and subtract ⅛in (3mm) from both the height and the width. Transfer these measurements on to the card, and cut it to size with the sharp knife.

Velvet material can be purchased from a fabric shop. You should buy enough of it to cover the entire card, with sufficient margin on each of the four edges to fold around the back. Cut away the corners of the material, so that it tucks neatly behind in the form of mitre joins. Apply contact adhesive to the card, and to the rear surface of the velvet, turning the

The small brass plate used to mount the cabinet to the wall is set into a shallow recess cut on the rear edge of the top panel, and secured with screws.

edges so that they each fold around the card and stick down flat. Then brush more adhesive on to the inside surface of the back panel, and to the rear surface of the velvet-covered board. Press the lined backing in place to make a permanent bond.

Measure the exact distance between each of the three pairs of shelving slots, together with the depth as far back as the velvet lining, and take these measurements to your local glazing supplier. Ask for three pieces of glass to be cut from 4mm-thick clear glass, and have the front edges polished to remove any sharpness which might cause nasty cuts to the fingers at some later stage when the cabinet is in use. Check that the glass shelves fit by sliding them into their grooves.

Finally, with the shelves removed, fit a small brass mounting plate to the middle of the top panel's rear edge. A shallow recess will have to be chiselled out before the plate can be screwed flush with the edge. Replace the glass shelves, and the cabinet is ready to be hung from a 1in (25mm) number 6 woodscrew driven into the wall of your room.

19 The Mantelpiece

CUTTING LIST

Mantelshelf: one of 54 × 6¾ × ¾in (1,372 × 172 × 19mm)

Cornice rail: one of 50 × 4¾ × 1¼in (1,270 × 121 × 32mm)

Crosspanel: one of 36¾ × 6¾ × ¾in (933 × 172 × 19mm)

Bottom rail: one of 36¾ × 2¾ × ¾in (933 × 72 × 19mm)

Column front panel: two of 44¾ × 5¾ × ¾in (1,137 × 146 × 19mm)

Column side panel: four of 44¾ × 2¾ × ¾in (1,137 × 70 × 19mm)

Long skirting board: two of 7¼ × 6¾ × ¾in (184 × 172 × 19mm)

Short skirting board: four of 4¼ × 6¾ × ¾in (108 × 172 × 19mm)

Long decorative panel: one of 33 × 4 × ¼in (838 × 100 × 6mm)

Short decorative panel: two of 3¼ × 4 × ¼in (82 × 100 × 6mm)

Batten: two of 36 × ⅞ × ⅞in (915 × 22 × 22mm)

Lengths of quadrant and astragal moulding

CONSTRUCTION

The fireplace is traditionally the main feature of the lounge or living room, and the mantelpiece that surrounds it is an important item of decoration. There are many variations on the classic mantelpiece design, but the basic structure is usually the same. It consists of a mantelshelf supported at each end by an ornamented column, both the columns being joined by a rail which lies directly beneath the shelf, and the crosspanel below that. The ornamentation mostly takes the form of additional panelling, or carving, fluting to the columns, and moulded strips which divide the mantelpiece into clearly defined sections.

Begin by selecting the wood. There is a wide range from which you can make your choice, depending on the type of finish you want. For instance, the softwoods yield parana pine, an excellent light brown timber with a smooth, even texture which could be either painted or given a clear gloss finish. Then there are the high-quality hardwoods like afrormosia, utile and oak. My choice here is utile, which is similar to sapele in its properties and therefore makes a useful substitute for mahogany.

The finished mantelpiece.

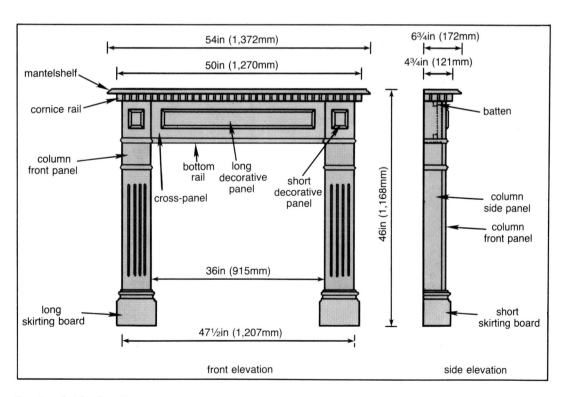

Front and side elevations.

The first step is to measure the cornice rail to length and mark in the dentils. A dentil pattern is a series of raised blocks separated by narrow recesses. There are two ways of making a dentil pattern: you can either cut out the blocks one by one from suitable matching material and glue them at regular intervals on to the front edge and the two ends of the rail, or you can cut the recesses into the rail itself. My method is to cut them in the rail. Each raised block is 1in (25mm) wide, the recess ¼in (6mm) wide and ¼in (6mm) deep. Clearly you will have to alter the overall length of the rail slightly so that it begins and ends with a dentil. The dentils may need to be enlarged on both ends of the rail, according to its exact width, but here they are not quite so prominent and any minor variation will hardly be noticed.

Mark in the series of lines with a square and pencil, and saw down each line to a depth of ¼in (6mm). You may prefer to clamp the rail in the vice, with its front edge facing uppermost, and make the cuts with the tenon saw; but it is quicker to clamp the rail to the end of the work-bench and make the series of cuts with the jigsaw. Chop out the waste with the ¼in (6mm) chisel.

The two vertical columns are attached to the underside of the cornice rail with housing joints; they consist of a front panel and two sides, which are all dowel-jointed together. For the time being, however, they are kept separate. The column's three components each have a bare-faced tenon which, when assembled, fits into a special U-shaped housing groove.

It is preferable to cut the tenons first, each being ½in (13mm) thick and ¾in (19mm) deep, scribing the lines with the marking gauge and cutting away the waste with the tenon saw. Now transfer the positions of the tenons on to the underside of the rail and mark in the corresponding grooves, checking that the two columns stand exactly 36in (915mm) apart from one another.

The easiest way of cutting the grooves is to use the electric router fitted with a ½in (13mm) straight cutter, or by taking two bites at it with a ¼in (6mm) cutter. The depth of the cut is set to fractionally more than ¾in (19mm), to accommodate the tenons. The alternative is to drill a series of holes and chop out the waste with the ½in (13mm) chisel, but the router gives a much faster and cleaner result.

Check the fitting of the joints. When you are satisfied that they mate perfectly, measure the crosspanel and the bottom

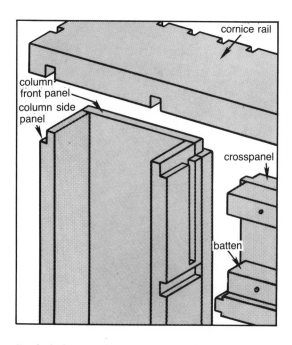

Exploded view of joints between cornice rail, column panels, crosspanel and bottom rail, including battens.

rail, allowing for the ⅜in (9mm) tongues to be cut at both ends of each piece to slot into housing grooves cut in the face of the two inner side panels of the columns. Mark in the positions of the grooves and cut them with the router. Measure and mark in the corresponding tongues in the crosspanel and bottom rail, cutting them to size with the tenon saw. The cross-panel is attached to the under-side of the top rail and the upper side of the bottom rail with a 1 × 1in (25 × 25mm) hard-wood batten. Each of the two battens has two rows of four countersunk holes drilled along adjacent edges to take 1½in (38mm) number 8 woodscrews.

Measure the mantelshelf and cut it to the required length. Clamp it securely to the work-bench and prepare a Roman ogee moulding along its two ends and the front edge with the router. The Roman ogee profile is an attractive S-shaped curve, and the cut entails removing a large amount of waste. Do not attempt to work the full cut in a single run, but make several passes of the router in a succession of steps, increasing the depth of the cut each time until you reach the desired profile. Prepare the two end-grains first, finishing along the direction of the grain. Rub down with medium-grade sandpaper.

Still working with the router, change the cutter to a semi-circular core box cut-ter of ½in (13mm) diameter, and prepare the four or five flutes on the surface of the two column front panels. First, deter-mine the limits of the fluting, and square in a pencil line to show where to start the routing and where to finish.

Decide how many flutes you want to make on each panel. For four flutes, measure the width of the front panel and divide it into five equal widths – five flutes would require six equal widths, and so on – to give the centre position for each flute. If you wish to create a wider flute than the width of the cutter will permit, simply adjust the fence of the router to move the cutter fractionally to one side, and take a second run.

To ensure that the router always starts and finishes at exactly the same place along the length of the panel, where the two pencil lines have been squared across, two pieces of scrap wood with straight edges should be clamped at right-angles to the grain in such a way that they act as an automatic stop for the router's circular base. Used in conjunc-tion with the adjustable fence, you can work the tool with absolute precision, so that all the flutings are parallel to each other and in perfect alignment top and bottom. Sandpaper inside the flutes with medium-grade paper to remove any slight grooves or ridges left by the pas-sing of the cutter.

Assemble the cornice rail to the under-side of the mantelshelf using glue and screws. Five 2in (50mm) number 10 woodscrews are sufficient to hold the two parts firmly together, arranging them at regular intervals along the bot-tom surface of the top rail, 2in (50mm) from the rear edge. Drill and countersink the holes in the rail, and drive in the screws until they just emerge on the other side. Now, with the two parts turned upside-down on the work-bench, lay the top rail on to the bottom surface of the mantelshelf, their rear edges flush with each other, and an equal overhang at either end. Holding the two parts tightly together, give all five screws one or two turns to make an impression on the mantelshelf. Then slacken them off and remove the rail.

The cornice rail is fastened to the mantelshelf with a series of five number 10 woodscrews.

There should now be a row of five holes, guiding you to the places where the same number 10 wood bit is used to drill ½in (13mm) down into the mantelshelf. Beware that you do not bore any deeper than that, otherwise you may rupture the top surface. Mix a quantity of wood glue, brush it on to the two adjoining surfaces, and screw the top rail to the mantelshelf. It is not necessary to clamp the two parts together, as the screws serve that purpose well enough.

The next task is to assemble the two columns, joining the sides to the front rail. Dowel joints are employed to attach the front edge of the side panels to the rear face of the front panel. These are further reinforced with strengthening blocks glued in place within the column.

To prepare the dowel joints, firstly mark the centre line along the length of the front edge for both the side panels, adjusting the marking gauge until its spur coincides with the point midway across the thickness of the material. Run the gauge along the entire length of the two edges. Then, without altering the setting of the gauge, scribe two lines on the rear face of the front panel so that each line corresponds precisely with the marking of the side panels.

I would recommend that you use five dowels per joint, spaced at intervals along the length of the panels. The two outermost dowels are set 4in (100mm) from the ends of each column, with the remaining three arranged at equal distances in between. Measure and mark in the position of all the dowel holes on the scribed lines. Drill all the holes with the ½in (13mm)-diameter centre bit. Those in the side panels should be 1in (25mm) deep, and those in the front panel, ½in (13mm) deep. Cut the dowels from ½in (13mm)-diameter material, each one measuring 1⅜in (35mm) in length. Before attempting to glue the joints together, place the dowels in their holes and assemble the panels to check the mating of the three components. If there must be any slight inaccuracy in forming the column, it would be preferable to err in favour of being too generous with the edges of the front panel, since these can be more easily planed down afterwards.

Mix a quantity of wood glue and apply it by brush to all joining surfaces, together with the dowels. Fit the two side panels to the front panel, tapping them fully home with the mallet if necessary, and check with the square that they form perfect right-angles.

One of the main problems with an assembly of this kind, which is long and has two surfaces joined simultaneously, is that at least six clamps would be needed to hold it firmly together, but most woodworkers usually possess only two or three G-clamps and two sash cramps. An alternative method is therefore needed. Fortunately, nothing more is required other than the flat surface of the work-bench, and a number of building bricks or concrete blocks, which are easily obtained. The assembled column is placed on the work-bench, with its front panel uppermost, and the bricks placed upon it to exert enough pressure to keep the assembled joints in close contact. Occasionally you will find that there is a natural spring in the wood used for the front panel, so that in certain places it does not seat properly on the edges of the side panels. Additional weight must be applied by loading more blocks in that area.

When the glue has dried completely, remove the weights. Measure the internal dimensions of the two columns, and cut six blocks from off-cut wood, three for each column. These must be cut to fit tightly, so you will either have to be very precise with your measuring, or make them marginally too big and trim them back until they slot in. As they are out of sight in the finished mantelpiece, it does not matter how they are arranged provided that one is set approximately 3in (75mm) from the top of the column, the next one placed half-way down, and the third 5in (125mm) from the bottom. Prepare more wood glue, apply it to both ends and one edge of each block, and fit all six into the two columns.

The main components of the mantelpiece now consist of the two columns, the mantelshelf with its cornice rail, the crosspanel and the bottom rail. Fit these all together temporarily, without glue, to check that they fit fully in with each other. Cut the battens to length and drill the two rows of countersunk number 8 holes, four holes per row. Fit the 1½in (38mm) woodscrews, place the battens in position where they butt up against the corners between the crosspanel and the two rails, and drive the screws partly in to make their mark. Dismantle the assembly and enlarge the marked screw hole positions with the brace and number 8 bit. Fit the battens to the top and bottom rails, gluing and screwing them in place.

The mantelpiece is now ready for final assembly. The task will prove much simpler if you have an assistant on hand to support the structure as it comes together. Mix a large quantity of wood glue in a cup and have a clean ½in (13mm) brush available to apply it quickly to all the joining surfaces. Holding both columns vertically, apply glue to the housing grooves cut on their inside surfaces, and fit the tongues of the crosspanel and the bottom rail. Next, glue the mortise and tenon joints between the tops of the columns and the under-side of the cornice rail, and tap the mantelshelf down into position. You will need to knock the joints fully home with the mallet, holding a clean block of scrap wood on top of the mantelshelf to absorb the blows and prevent its upper surface from being dented.

Once you are satisfied that all the joints are properly located, screw the two battens to the rear of the crosspanel. Re-

move any surplus glue, where it has squeezed out from the joints, by wiping it with a damp rag. Lay the mantelpiece structure on a perfectly flat floor while the glue dries and hardens.

Various types of decoration may be applied to the surface of the mantelpiece. For instance, lengths of quadrant moulding can be cut to fit in the corners between the crosspanel and the cornice rail, and the joins between the crosspanel and the two columns. It could also be run around the top of each column to conceal its join with the cornice rail, cutting mitre joints and attaching the pieces with wood glue.

Measure and cut lengths of astragal

Astragal moulding, cut with mitre joints at each end, is fixed to the columns and across the front edge of the bottom rail with wood glue and veneer pins.

moulding to fit along the front edge of the bottom rail, continuing it around both columns. A second layer is set 4in (100mm) lower down on each column. Mitre all corners and fix the strips in place with wood glue. It could be argued that the longer pieces should be attached with thin veneer pins as well as glue – and this might indeed prove necessary if there is a natural tendency for the moulding to bend. However, pins should be avoided if possible.

Three decorative panels are fitted to the front of the mantelpiece – a single long piece attached to the crosspanel, and two smaller pieces, each fitted in matching positions on the front of the columns, all three being at the same height. They are all cut from a length of ¼in (6mm) thick sapele, and all the edges are chamfered to make a more pleasing appearance. Each panel is fitted in place with glue, and once again veneer pins should only be used if the wood has a slight spring to it.

It is often the case with an old-fashioned design that the upper part of the mantelpiece is given some carved work to add decoration to the crosspanel and the front of the columns. It is up to you to decide whether carving will improve the appearance of the finished mantelpiece. If you are in favour of it, you can either try your hand at this most intricate craft, for which you will need to equip yourself with a range of special carving tools, or you can cheat a little and buy a variety of carved patterns produced on hardwood which are ready to glue in place.

The last item of trim to be attached to the main structure of the mantelpiece is the skirting boards which fit at the base of the two columns. It may be argued

that these are not strictly necessary, since fireplaces are often designed with the mantelpiece raised off the ground by a matter of several inches, resting on a marbled hearth, and therefore at a higher level than the rest of the room's skirting-boards. However, the presence of the boards, acting as a plinth for the base of each column, is a matter of correctness in classical architecture, so it is important to include them.

The material used for the skirting-boards should be the same as that used to make the rest of the mantelpiece – in this case, sapele. It will need a suitable moulding to be cut at the top, and this is a task that is best entrusted to your local timber merchant or joinery. Various mouldings can be made, based on standard patterns, and clearly you will need to use a traditional style for this particular purpose.

Having obtained a long length of skirting-board, you must measure carefully the lengths required for the three boards that must fit around the three external surfaces of each column. The corners are mitre-jointed where they meet at the two front corners of the colums, and likewise this is a piece of precision machine work which your wood supplier is better equipped to carry out than you are – provided you supply accurate column measurements.

You can, of course, attempt to cut your own mitres if you wish, but it is very hard to achieve total accuracy down the entire width of the board, especially with a hardwood, and unless you have a proper mitre-jig, the result will be far from satisfactory.

The three skirting-board components are fitted at the base of each column with glue and screws. The screws are all driven through from the inside of the columns, so that their heads are not visible, and this entails drilling a series of holes through the front and side panels. Four holes are bored in the front panel, and two in each of the side panels. Those in the front panel are drilled perpendicularly to the surface, but the holes that pass through the sides are set at an angle, to permit access for the drill and the screwdriver. Even so, it will not be possible to use a handbrace, owing to the sweep of the handle, and the drilling must be carried out either using the hand drill or the electric drill. Countersink all the holes.

Mix a quantity of wood glue, and firstly apply it by brush to the rear surface of the front skirting-board. Place this in position and hold it firmly to the column with two G-clamps. Fit four 1in (25mm) number 8 woodscrews in their holes and drive them fully home. When the glue has dried completely, carry out the same procedure for the two side skirting-boards, gluing them tightly up against the front board to form a perfect right-angled mitre joint, and screw them in place. On this occasion, due to the screw holes passing at an angle through the wood, you can safely use 1½in (38mm) number 8 woodscrews without the risk of the tip emerging on the surface of the boards.

It only remains to fit two small brass fixing plates to the rear edge of each column, one at the top and one at the bottom. These four plates are responsible for securing the mantelpiece to the wall of the chimney-piece. They can be purchased from your local ironmongery shop, together with a supply of 1in (25mm) number 6 fixing screws. Place each plate in the required position on the rear edge of each column's outermost side panel, the top pair set down 6in (150mm) from the mantelshelf, the bottom pair set up 6in (150mm) from the base, and mark around them in pencil. Cut out a shallow recess with a chisel to allow all four plates to fit flush with the surface of the wood, then mark in the screw holes. Drill the holes with a number 6 bit, and drive in the screws until the plates are securely attached.

Rub down all surfaces of the mantelpiece with medium-grade sandpaper, always working the abrasive paper in the direction of the grain, and paying particular attention to all joints where glue may have squeezed out during assembly and spread across the surface. All traces must be completely removed. Fill any small gaps between the joints with wood stopper. When this has dried to a hard cake, rub it down with sandpaper, switching from medium to fine-grade.

Choose a wood stain to match your desired colour. With a material such as sapele, with its close affinity to mahogany, the most appropriate shade is the reddish brown of a mahogany dye. Apply this thoroughly to all visible surfaces with a brush, allowing the first treatment to dry completely before applying the second. There may be a difference in the colour of natural sapele and that of the hardwood used for the astragal and quadrant mouldings, but a third application given to the lighter-coloured wood with a small artist's paintbrush should blend it well enough with the darker material. Once the stain has dried, give the mantelpiece at least two coats of mahogany-coloured varnish, which will add further to the dye already applied, and provide the surface of the wood with a satisfying shine.

An alternative type of finish which will prove equally acceptable is a coloured wood treatment, which contains an oily substance and is usually employed to protect the surface in outdoor surroundings; several coats will build up a rich, glowing sheen, and any difference in the original colour of the wood should be brought to a single uniform shade.

In case you are worried that these wood treatments, some of which contain highly inflammable substances, could prove to be a fire hazard, it should be pointed out that they are at their most volatile whilst they are in liquid form, and therefore the greatest risk is during the period when they are being applied to the wood. However, the treatment is given to the mantelpiece in the workshop where adequate ventilation can be provided by opening doors and windows. The vapour gradually disperses as the substances dry.

Special attention must be given to the fitting of the mantelpiece. Depending on the type of fire installed in the grate, the woodwork must never be allowed to get very hot.

20 The Music Cabinet

CUTTING LIST

Lid: one of 24⅞ × 19¼ × ⅞in (632 × 489 × 22mm)

Base: one of 24⅞ × 19¼ × ⅞in (632 × 489 × 22mm)

Side panel: two of 9 × 18¾ × ¾in (229 × 476 × 19mm)

Front drawer panel: one of 22 × 8½ × ¾in (559 × 216 × 19mm)

Top back rail: one of 22⅞ × 1½ × ¾in (582 × 38 × 19mm)

Bottom back rail: one of 22⅞ × 1 × ¾in (582 × 25 × 19mm)

Back panel: two of 22⅝ × 3¾ × ⅜in (575 × 95 × 9mm)

Leg: four of 21 × 1¾ × 1¾in (533 × 45 × 45mm)

Front and back top rail: two of 23⅝ × 3⅜ × ¾in (600 × 86 × 19mm)

Side top rail: two of 18⅛ × 3⅜ × ¾in (460 × 86 × 19mm)

Front and back bottom rail: two of 23⅝ × 1¼ × ¾in (600 × 32 × 19mm)

Side bottom rail: two of 18⅛ × 1¼ × ¾in (460 × 32 × 19mm)

Bottom shelf: one of 24¾ × 19⅛ × ½in (628 × 486 × 13mm)

Corner joining block: four of 4 × 4 × 1¼in (100 × 100 × 32mm)

CONSTRUCTION

It is not very often that the cabinet-maker gets the chance to work with mature mahogany, which is a rich, finely-grained hardwood with a distinctive reddish colour, widely regarded as one of the most perfect materials for high-quality cabinet work.

For certain kinds of reproduction-style furniture, it may be argued that Spanish mahogany, which comes from the West Indies, or Honduras mahogany from Central America, are the only correct materials to use; and none of the derivative woods such as sapele or utile compare on equal terms, even if there is more than a passing resemblance. The colour of these similar woods is usually more of a light brown, and the grain is less well figured.

However, mahogany is not easy to obtain, and its scarcity makes it very expensive; so there has to be an alternative means of acquiring it. An excellent source of well-seasoned hardwood is the second-hand furniture market, and if you search hard enough you can have a few pleasant surprises. The consignment of mahogany used to illustrate this chapter came from a garden shed, where it had been languishing for a number of years gathering dust. In its former days, it had existed as the top of a large drop-leaf table, and consisted of three boards. The first of these was in particularly good condition, with the original finish still intact, but the other two had deteriorated badly, with spots of paint and ingrained mud covering them.

The usual procedure with salvaged wood is to take it to a local joinery where for a small fee the boards are fed through a planing machine to skim off the top surface, thus revealing fresh grain free from all the original surface imperfections. The machining process obviously requires you to take off all the old iron-mongery and remove any screws or nails. There is also a limit to the width of board that can be passed through the planer – normally around 20in (508mm) – so you must first cut the boards roughly to size.

The music cabinet is constructed in two parts. The cabinet itself comprises of a simple box-type structure, with a top lid that hinges upwards, and a front panel, made to resemble a drawer, which hinges downwards. The combined effect is to provide plenty of access to the interior of the cabinet so that it can be used to house a record player. The second part of the structure is the leg framework upon which the cabinet stands and to which it is permanently attached.

Once the boards have been planed, but before they are cut any further, check

The finished music cabinet.

that the internal dimensions of the cabinet are sufficient to accommodate your record player, not only in terms of width and depth, but also height. It may be necessary to increase the measurements of the example given here.

The lid and the base of the cabinet are identical in every respect, and they each have a Roman ogee profile worked along the front edge and two end-grains. This edging process is best carried out with the electric router fitted with the appropriate cutter. Firstly, measure and mark both panels to the specified width, and cut them carefully to size with the jigsaw, planing both end-grains and edges straight and square.

Place the Roman ogee cutter in the router, and set the depth gauge to give the desired edge profile. Starting with the end-grains, and taking the usual precaution of clamping a piece of waste in

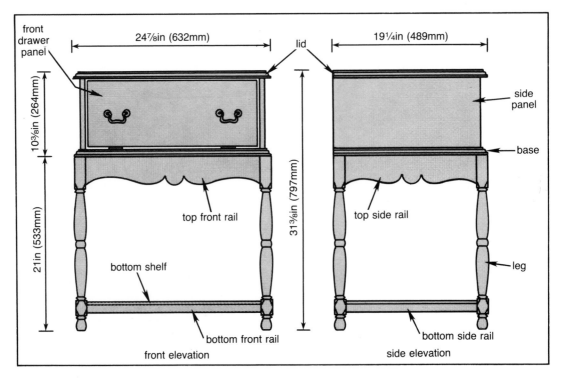

front
drawer
panel

24⅞in (632mm)

lid

19¼in (489mm)

side
panel

base

10⅜in (264mm)

21in (533mm)

31⅜in (797mm)

top front rail

top side rail

bottom shelf

leg

bottom front rail

bottom side rail

front elevation

side elevation

Front and side elevations.

position at the end of the router's travel to prevent the wood from splitting, make a series of runs commencing with a shallow cut and increasing the depth of the cutting blade until it reaches its lowest position. If you were to attempt to make the cut in a single run of the router, the blade would meet great resistance and overheat, causing the wood to scorch, whereas several runs will remove only a little waste at a time, and result in a far more satisfactory finish. When both sides are complete, make the final router cut along the front edge. Rub down all three profiles with fine sandpaper to remove the fine strands of wood.

The next stage is to cut the two side panels and joint them to the base; but firstly a word of explanation. In any box-type cabinet of this kind, it is usual to arrange for the grain to run in a vertical direction. As a rule, it would follow that the only technically correct method of fitting a solid back panel would be to fit it with the direction of its grain matching that of the adjoining sides, so that if there were to be any shrinkage in the wood, it would take place uniformly without causing splits. However, this would inevitably mean setting the hinges for the lid into the end-grain of the back panel, which is not advisable because its fixing screws will not take hold properly when they are driven in thus.

Instead, the back of the cabinet is built up from two rails, one placed at the top, the other at the bottom. In between these rails, and set inside specially cut grooves, are two thin panels of mahogany, arranged so that their grain runs horizon-

Cutting the groove in the base to receive the bottom back rail. The two mortises for the side panels have already been prepared using the same router method.

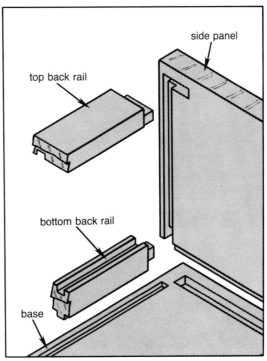

Exploded view of joints.

tally, in keeping with the rails. By fitting the panels loosely inside the grooves, with a thin gap separating them, any movement of the wood will be absorbed and no stress will be put on it.

The two side panels are fitted to the base with long mortise and tenon joints. First, measure and cut each panel to size, allowing an extra ⅜in (9mm) to its length for the tenon that must be cut along the bottom edge. To mark out the mortise at each end of the base panel, set the spurs of the mortise gauge to a gap of ⅜in (9mm) and scribe the two pairs of parallel lines in the required positions so that the sides are both set in by ¼in (6mm) from the innermost part of the Roman ogee moulding. Set in the ends of the two mortises by ½in (13mm) front and back.

The only practical way of cutting out the two mortises without damaging the nearby end-grain and splitting the wood

is to use the router, this time fitting it with a straight-tipped cutter. On the face of it, you might think that the best size of cutter to make a ⅜in (9mm)-wide channel is one that has a diameter of ⅜in (9mm), working it in a single run. In fact, this method will work most satisfactorily if you align the router correctly – but there is no room for error.

By fitting a ¼in (6mm)-diameter cutter, you not only facilitate an easier run by reducing the resistance in the wood, you also provide yourself with more room, so that you make your first cut down the centre of the marked area. The cutter should then be moved slightly to one side, and then the other, to complete the job. This gives you perfect control over the placing of the finished mortise.

To ensure that the router follows a

straight line for the duration of the cut, it is best to remove the adjustable fence completely so that the base of the router can be placed flat on the surface of the workpiece. Clamp a strip of straight-edged batten along the panel, from front to back, thereby acting as a guide. Obviously you will have to make very fine alterations to its position, checking along the entire length of the marked area, before you switch on the router and make your first cut. Once the batten has been correctly located and firmly clamped, it makes for a very accurate guide indeed.

When the two mortises have been cut, and the semi-circular ends chopped square with the ⅜in (9mm) chisel, the next task is to prepare the tenons along the bottom end-grain of the two side panels. Likewise, these are best cut with the router, using the same principle of clamping a piece of straight-edged batten along the panel to act as a guide. This is different from the customary way of cutting a tenon, using the tenon saw, for the simple reason that the joint runs over a considerable length relative to its thickness.

The marking-out is done in the usual way with the mortise gauge, keeping the gap between the spurs to ⅜in (9mm), and adjusting the fence so that the two lines are scribed centrally across the end-grain. With the marking gauge, scribe a single line on each side to indicate the shoulders, which are set to a depth of ⅜in (9mm). As in the instance above, the same ¼in (6mm) cutter is probably the best size to use, making two runs with the router for each shoulder.

The tenon must now be set in at each end to match the length of the mortise, noting that the rear edges lie flush when the side is joined to the base panel. Trim the second pair of shoulders with the tenon saw, and experimentally fit each side to the base, tapping them fully home with the mallet.

The two back rails come next. These are fitted to the two side panels with mortise and tenon joints, and it is wise to make both the rails somewhat greater in length than you actually need. The top rail has a groove cut along its lower side to receive the back panel, and the lower rail has a matching groove cut in its upper edge, as well as having a tongue worked along its lower edge to fit into a groove cut along the rear surface of the base; the surplus lengths permit the grooves and tongue to be cut without the risk of over-cutting at the start and finish, since these are trimmed off later.

The top rail is mounted in such a way that its width is 1½in (38mm) and its height ¾in (19mm), to allow enough room for the lid hinges to be attached; whereas the bottom rail is placed with its width equal to ¾in (19mm) and its height, 1in (25mm) including the tongue. The grooves and tongue are all cut in a similar fashion to the method used for the mortise and tenon joints employed for the side panels and the base. It should be noted that the grooves for the back panels are cut to a depth of ¼in (6mm) in the top and bottom rails, and are set in by ¼in (6mm) from the rear edge. Grooves are likewise cut on the inside faces of the two side panels, and stopped ½in (13mm) short from the ends.

With the side panels fitted fully in their joints, place a square on the base and make any slight adjustments to their positions so that they form perfect right-angles with the base panel. Measure the distance between the inside faces of the two sides at the rear where the rails are to be fitted, one measurement taken at the top and one at the bottom. These distances ought to be exactly the same.

The rails are fitted to the side panels with mortise and tenon joints. In the case of the bottom rail, the mortise is quite narrow, with a width of ¼in (6mm), and is arranged to fit into a deepened part of the back panel groove already cut. The top rail has a bare-faced tenon which is set in by ¼in (6mm) from the rear edge, so that it incorporates part of the back panel groove. The mortise is cut to match, and chopping out the waste must be carried out with extreme care to avoid splitting the surrounding wood.

Cut the two back panels from mahogany which has been planed down to a thickness of ⅜in (9mm). When slotted into their grooves in the top and bottom back rails and the two side rails, there should still be a gap of ¹⁄₁₆in (2mm) or so separating them. Holes will eventually need to be drilled in the back panels to allow electrical flex and loudspeaker wires from the record player to be passed through, but this is left until later. Rub down the various component parts thoroughly with medium and fine-grade sandpaper to smooth the surfaces.

Mix a quantity of wood glue, and fit the bottom back rail to the base. Apply glue to the remaining joints and tap the two side panels loosely into their mortises. Place the two back panels in their grooves and finally fit the top back rail, knocking the whole assembly together. Cramp up the joints for at least a day whilst the glue dries and hardens. When sufficient time has elapsed, remove the cramps and repeat the rubbing down with sandpaper.

Cut the front drawer panel to size from a piece of mahogany so that it just fits within the opening between the sides, the lid and the base.

The second part of the music cabinet consists of the leg framework. The wood used for this supporting structure should ideally be the same as that employed for the cabinet. However, unless the original source of mahogany proved sufficiently generous, and included pieces with a cross-section of approximately 1¾ × 1¾in (45 × 45mm), you will have to look elsewhere for it. An excellent source of old mahogany is the timber salvage dealer who obtains a wide selection of hardwoods from many sources, which can be as diverse as the breaking of ships to the demolishing of buildings. Should it prove impossible to get hold of enough mahogany, the legs and their rails can be made from sapele or utile, which bear a reasonably close resemblance to mahogany.

The turning of the four legs inevitably entails lathe-work. Although woodturning is a craft in itself, here it plays a subordinate role. The lathe attachment for an electric drill is an ideal piece of equipment. You simply screw it firmly to the top of the work-bench and use your electric drill to provide the motive power. But if you have access to a full-sized lathe, so much the better. Occasionally, an obliging local joinery can be persuaded to let you work on its machinery during a slack period for a modest consideration – in which case you are advised to check the question of insurance cover – or it might be worth signing up for an evening class to get your hands on the workshop lathe!

The art of woodturning is not difficult to pick up, at least not for this type of work. The tools needed for the job are a set of three implements: spindle gouge, skew chisel and parting tool. These can be purchased in a set. You will also need protective spectacles to shield the eyes from flying splinters, and it is wise to wear ear-muffs.

Before the wood can be turned, it must be measured and cut to length. At this stage, it does not matter whether it is sawn or planed. It should be 20¾in (527mm) long, and 1¾ × 1¾in (45 × 45mm) in cross-section. Mark and cut the ends square.

Find the point at the centre of each end-grain by drawing two diagonal lines with the pencil and rule. Place the tip of the bradawl at the intersection of these lines, and make a small pilot hole. Remove the conical-shaped tailstock from the lathe and drive the tip into the pilot hole by tapping it hard with the mallet. Likewise, take the drive component from the headstock and knock this into the end-grain at the opposite end. The length of wood can now be securely mounted in the lathe.

When the entire length of wood is to be turned into a cylindrical shape, it is usual to plane down the four corners of the piece so that it takes on an octagonal shape when viewed in cross-section, thus easing the impact of the spinning wood upon the spindle gouge. But this is not possible with the cabinet legs, because a short section at the top and bottom must remain square. The actual amount left untouched for these sections is 4in (100mm) at the top and 5in (125mm) at the bottom, of which, in the latter case, the lower half is turned to form the foot.

Mark in these limits along the length of the wood, squaring around the piece in thick pencil so that the lines stand out clearly when the lathe is rotating at high speed. The first step is to rough out the cylinder using the spindle gouge. The extreme ends of the cylinder may be cut square with the parting tool. Next, measure and mark in the points where the major changes in the pattern occur. Once again, these will need clear pencil lines which are then converted into shallow depressions with the tip of the parting tool. You do not have to copy the profile of the legs as shown in our example, but it is advisable to adhere to one particular established pattern.

If this is your first attempt at wood-turning, you should practise on a piece of scrap wood, preferably of the same material as that used for the four legs, whether it be mahogany or sapele, until you have perfected the technique of holding the spindle gouge or parting tool against the tool rest of the lathe and applying just enough pressure to remove the waste in a clean cutting motion. It is a technique that cannot be described, only felt.

In the absence of a proper vernier gauge, a pair of geometrical compasses or dividers must be used to measure the diameter of the cylinder in its various parts where changes take place, and check that the proportions are symmetrical from the centre outwards. It is not easy to copy exactly the same contours in all four legs, especially when you are new to the task of woodturning, and it is not unusual to find that the last of the legs is noticeably better than the first.

The answer is to place each leg back in the lathe and turn it to remove a little more from the curves until all four are identical. At this stage, you should also turn the foot at the base of the leg. Finally, with the leg still spinning in the lathe, hold a piece of fine-grade sand-paper against the turned sections to smooth and further refine the surface finish. Friction will cause the sandpaper to get very hot, so take care not to burn your fingers.

To complete the leg, clamp it horizontally in the vice with the pressure of the jaws bearing against the unturned square section at the top end of the leg, and plane down the four flat faces equally until they lie within $\frac{1}{16}$in (2mm) of the nearest turning. Reverse the leg in the vice to repeat the same operation on the small square section above the foot. At both these points, the leg should measure $1\frac{5}{8} \times 1\frac{5}{8}$in (41 × 41mm) in cross-section. The legs are now ready to be joined to the rails.

The four top rails are wide enough to have their bottom edges decorated with a pattern of curves, though in fact the back rail is out of sight and is left with a straight bottom edge. The four bottom rails are much narrower, and serve only to support the shelf. Each rail is attached to the legs with mortise and tenon joints, the main difference in the method of assembly between the two sizes being that the top rails are mounted with their outer sides practically flush with the outside edges of the legs, set in by a mere $\frac{1}{16}$in (2mm), whilst the bottom rails are located midway across the thickness of the legs.

In practice, this means that there is a difference in the way the joints are cut. For the bottom rails, conventional stopped mortise and tenon joints are employed; but because the top rails are set so closely to the outer edges of the legs, the same kind of joint in this case would be flawed either by a tenon that was too narrow or a mortise that was placed perilously adjacent to the edge of the wood. The solution is to fit the top rails with bare-faced tenons. In both cases, the mortises are cut to a depth of 1in (25mm).

In all other respects, the joints are marked and cut in the same fashion. The rails are all $\frac{3}{4}$in (19mm) thick, so the top mortise and bare-faced tenon are each set to a width of $\frac{1}{2}$in (13mm), with the mortise positioned $\frac{5}{16}$in (8mm) from the outer edge of the leg. The bottom mortise and tenon is similarly $\frac{1}{2}$in (13mm) wide, but is placed centrally across the thickness of the leg. The top joints are all set in by $\frac{1}{2}$in (13mm) from the edges of the rail, the bottom joints being set in by only $\frac{1}{4}$in (6mm).

Cut all the rails to the required length, allowing 1in (25mm) at each end for the tenon. Mark a curved pattern for the front and side rails on to two separate pieces of card, drawing the lines with a pair of compasses and art stencils. Two templates are needed because the front rail is longer than the two sides, so the curves must be drawn in the correct proportion.

Cut the templates carefully with the sharp knife, and transfer the patterns on to the wood. Remove the bulk of the waste with the jigsaw or coping saw, working the blade close to the pencil line but slightly on the waste side of it. Clamp each piece in the vice and complete the shaping of the curves with the spokeshave. The rear top rail, having no curves, is prepared from planed wood measuring $3\frac{3}{8} \times \frac{3}{4}$in (87 × 19mm); the bottom rails are all cut from material that measures $1\frac{1}{4} \times \frac{3}{4}$in (32 × 19mm).

Mark in all the mortises with the mortise gauge, remembering that there are two different settings for the top and bottom rails, in so far as the top mortises are set ⅝₁₆in (8mm) from the outer edge while the bottom rails are placed dead centre. Chop them out in the usual manner. Mark the tenons likewise, removing the waste with the tenon saw.

Make a test fitting of all the joints, checking that they each fit fully home. Temporarily assemble the leg framework to ensure that all the corners are square and that the structure stands with all four feet resting on a level surface, and does not rock. This is a very important detail if the finished music cabinet is to house a record player, which can be affected by the slightest movement.

Any unevenness may be corrected by trimming a small amount from the bottom of one or more of the feet, until they are all of exactly the same length. The offending leg can simply be mounted

back in the lathe and turned again, using the parting tool to pare off a tiny amount from the end of the foot.

Next, cut the corner blocks to size from 4 × 1¼in (100 × 32mm) wood. This need not be mahogany or sapele, but should be a hardwood. Off-cuts such as ash or beech would be quite suitable. These corner blocks serve two functions: they give added strength to the framework, and they provide the means of attaching it to the underside of the cabinet. Each block consists of a triangle with a square portion removed from the apex, to fit around the leg. As there will inevitably be a slight variation between one corner and the other three, all the blocks must be made-to-measure.

Prepare the leg framework for assembly. Rub down all the rails with medium

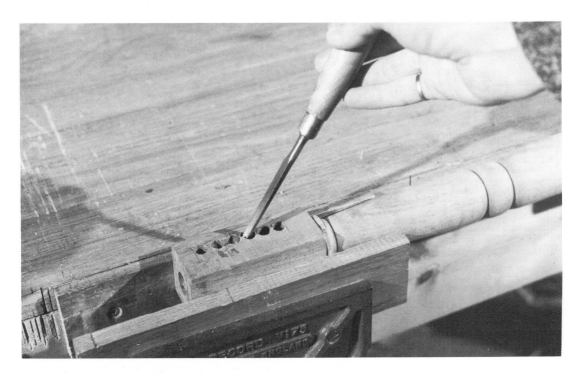

Chopping out the mortise at the top of the leg.

The front top rail of the leg framework is fitted to the leg with a mitred mortise and tenon joint.

and fine-grade sandpaper. Mix a quantity of wood glue and assemble the rails to the legs, tapping all the joints lightly with the mallet so that they fit perfectly together. Wipe away any excess glue from around the joints with a damp rag, and cramp up the assembly for at least a day.

When the glue has set hard, take off the cramps and prepare to fit the four corner blocks. These are screwed in place, each block having two screws, one per rail, driven in diagonally. Start by drilling and countersinking the holes in the block, using the handbrace fitted with a number 8 drill bit, then place the block in position flush with the upper edge of the top rails and the end-grain of the leg, and mark the screw holes on the inside faces of the rails. Make a careful note of the diagonal path of the hole in the block, pencilling in a line along the top edge of the rail to signify a continu-

ation of it, thus giving the correct alignment of the drill.

Lay the leg framework flat on the work-bench, and manipulate the hand-brace with its number 8 bit to bore holes a short distance into the wood. The combined effect of the drilling should be to make holes to take 1½in (38mm) number 8 woodscrews. Finally, drill a number 8 hole through each of the corner blocks, somewhere near its centre, and countersink the under-side.

Prepare more wood glue, apply it to the abutting surfaces between the corner blocks, the legs and the rails, and fit all four blocks in place, making the fixture secure by driving in the screws. When the glue has completely dried, the leg framework can be joined to the cabinet. Turn the cabinet upside-down on a flat surface and, with the leg framework also inverted, place this carefully on the under-side of the base so that the four edges and corners of the legs align with the corners of the base. Mark the positions of the four screw holes through the corner blocks on to the base using the bradawl.

Remove the leg framework, and drill holes into the base with the number 8 drill bit to a depth of no more than ½in (13mm). Apply wood glue to the upper side of the four corner blocks, and along the top edge of the four top rails, and screw the leg framework to the cabinet with four 2in (50mm) number 8 woodscrews.

Cut eight pieces of scrap wood each measuring 2in (50mm) in length and triangular in cross-section. This may be achieved by cutting a single piece of material to a length of 8in (200mm) and planing it down until it measures ¾ × ¾in (19 × 19mm) in cross-section. Saw this up into four equal 2in (50mm) pieces, then cut these in half across their diagonal on the end-grain by placing them upright in the vice and sawing down with the tenon saw, thus creating two triangles. Brush wood glue on to the two right-angled edges and fit the blocks tightly up against the four inside corners formed between the four top rails and the base panel, arranging them two per rail, spaced apart at regular intervals. Their purpose is to strengthen the attachment of the cabinet to the legs.

The bottom shelf should be cut, if possible, from the same material as that used for the lid and the base of the cabinet, such as the old table tops. However, providence often decrees that what it supplied in such apparent abundance at the start of the work has by now dwindled to nothing. If there is not enough of the original wood left, you can make up a shelf by jointing two or three mahogany boards edge to edge. The best type of joint is undoubtedly the tongue and groove – in other words, the housing joint.

Firstly, have the boards planed down to a thickness of ½in (13mm). Set the spurs of the mortise gauge to a gap of ¼in (6mm), and score two parallel lines centrally along the abutting edges of each board. The groove is cut in the edge of the first board by channelling out the entire centre portion to a depth of ¼in (6mm), using the plough plane, and the tongue cut correspondingly in the second board by rebating the top and bottom sides to the same depth, so that the tongue slots fully into the groove.

Apply wood glue to the two parts of the joint, then fit them together and hold under pressure with cramps while the glue dries, ensuring that the resulting board is perfectly flat. When the cramps are later removed, measure and cut the shelf panel to size so that it overlaps the bottom rails and lies almost flush with the outer edges of the legs. It will be necessary to measure and cut out square-shaped portions from the four corners so that the shelf can fit around the legs. Round off the top edges of the shelf by rubbing with sandpaper, wrapping a sheet of medium-grade paper around a block of wood and working it in long strokes to ensure that each of the four edges is given equal treatment.

Cut a further ten triangular joining blocks, each the same size as those prepared earlier, and, with a supply of wood glue, attach the shelf in position. Apply the glue along the top edge of the four bottom rails, bring the shelf into contact, and hold it down firmly with G-clamps. Turning the entire cabinet assembly upside-down, glue the ten joining blocks into the four corners between the underside of the bottom shelf and the inner face of the rails, arranging them so that there are three triangular blocks to each of the longer rails, and two to each of the shorter rails, spacing them at regular intervals.

The lid is hinged to the cabinet with two 3in (75mm) brass butt hinges, and the false drawer front drops down on a pair of 2in (50mm) brass butt hinges, all of which are set in 2½in (63mm) from the sides. Both pairs of hinges are suitably rebated. A small brass cabinet lock is fitted in a recess cut centrally along the top inside face of the drawer front, and a key-hole bored out with a ⅜in (9mm) diameter centre bit, and sawn with the coping saw. A brass escutcheon is inserted into the key-hole on the outer side of the false drawer to serve as a liner.

Triangular corner blocks are fitted to the inside corners between the four legs and the top rails.

A pair of brass drawer handles are fitted half-way up the height of the drawer, each set 3in (75mm) from the end. Measure carefully for the attachment holes, and drill them out with a ¹⁄₁₆in (2mm)-diameter twist drill. The handles are fastened in place with small round-headed bolts which pass through from the inside face.

In the closed position, the lid may be kept shut by attaching a small sliding brass bolt on either side which slips into a receiver hole drilled on the inside face of each side panel. To secure the drawer front, it will be necessary to glue two thin wooden battens as drawer stops immediately behind the panel when it is in the

fully closed upright position, one on each side and mounted vertically. These battens are butt-jointed, and tacked with tiny veneer pins. Cut a narrow mortise on the under-side of the lid to receive the cabinet lock.

To complete the ensemble, the lid is furnished with a pair of stay brackets, one for each side, which are attached to the inside face of the two side panels and the under-side of the lid. These are fitted to prevent the lid from dropping shut every time it is opened. The stay brackets are made from brass, and in the folded position they measure approximately 8in (200mm) long. Although it may appear that the placing of these brackets is a

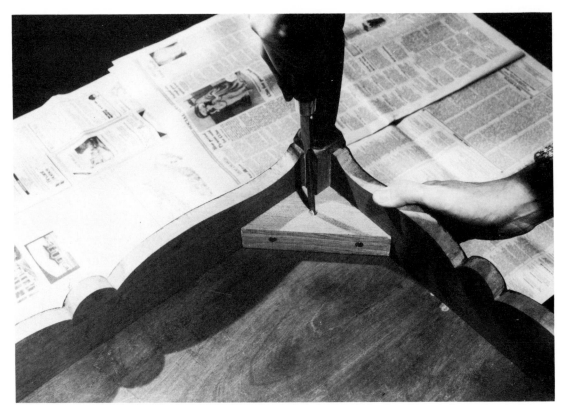

The leg framework is screwed to the under-side of the cabinet base through the four corner blocks.

somewhat arbitrary business, it is important to get the geometry right otherwise they will tend to open out of synchronisation.

If the finished cabinet is to have a practical purpose, place the record player inside it to determine precisely where the small holes must be drilled in the back panel for the electrical power flex and loudspeaker wires to pass through. Measure and mark the positions of the holes then, with a second person available to hold a block of scrap wood firmly against the inner side of the back panel, drill through from the outside with a ⅝in (16mm) centre bit. If the flex and the wires are all located close together, it would probably be simpler to cut out a single square or rectangular opening using the coping saw.

Remove the pair of drawer handles, and rub down all the surfaces thoroughly with very fine sandpaper before applying mahogany wood stain. This can be put on with either a brush or a soft cloth. In the former case, the stain will appear much stronger in colour, due to the fact that more of it is carried by the brush on to the wood, and therefore this method is recommended where the cabinet and the legs are made from more than one variety of mahogany or sapele, because any differences in the natural colour of the wood will be more effectively hidden.

When the same hardwood has been used throughout the construction, the wood stain is better applied with a cloth, since there is less chance of the liquid running and causing uneven patches. Two or three applications of stain will be required, each one being permitted to dry completely before the next is given.

Finally, the surfaces must be polished. French polish is the one to choose if you wish for the cabinet to posses a rich, glowing shine. It requires a high degree of skill in its application if the result is to be successful. The real secret is not to apply too much polish at a time. In between coats, when the polish has dried, give the surface a rub down with very fine wire wool soaked in white spirit. The alternative is to give the cabinet a thorough application of good-quality wax polish, but it should be noted that this does not produce such a high shine as French polish.

21 The Garden Seat

CUTTING LIST

Rear leg: two of 36 × 3¾ × 2½in (915 × 95 × 63mm)

Front leg: two of 23¼ × 5 × 2½in (592 × 126 × 63mm)

Arm-rest: two of 21½ × 2½ × 2½in (546 × 63 × 63mm)

Side seat rail: two of 18¼ × 2¾ × 1¾in (464 × 700 × 45mm)

Mid-seat rail: one of 18¼ × 2½ × 1¼in (464 × 63 × 32mm)

Lower side rail: two of 18¼ × 2½ × 1¼in (464 × 63 × 32mm)

Upper back-rest rail: one of 58¼ × 2¾ × 1¾in (1,480 × 70 × 45mm)

Lower back-rest rail: one of 58¼ × 2¾ × 1¾in (1,480 × 70 × 45mm)

Front seat rail: one of 58¼ × 3¾ × 1¾in (1,480 × 95 × 45mm)

Back seat rail: one of 58¼ × 2¾ × 1¾in (1,480 × 70 × 45m))

Wide back-rest slat: two of 12 × 4¾ × ⅞in (305 × 120 × 22mm)

Narrow back-rest slat: twelve of 12 × 1¾ × ⅞in (305 × 45 × 22mm)

Seat slat: four of 58¼ × 2½ × 1¼in (1,480 × 63 × 32mm)

32 dowel pegs, each measuring 2 × ¼in (50 × 6mm) diameter

CONSTRUCTION

The garden seat has an ageless and charming character of its own, bestowed upon it by a classical design and a method of construction that depends entirely on the mortise and tenon joint to ensure maximum strength and solidity. With the right timber and well-cut joints, the seat will last for years.

Before you begin on the seat, two important points need to be considered.

The first of these is to decide what type of wood you should use. This is often rather a difficult decision to make, because you have to balance cost against quantity – not an easy equation at the best of times. The most obvious and desirable choice is unquestionably oak, a hardwood ideally suited by virtue of its extremely tough and durable nature. But oak is now very expensive, and the amount required to build a large seat would certainly cost a lot of money.

The finished garden seat.

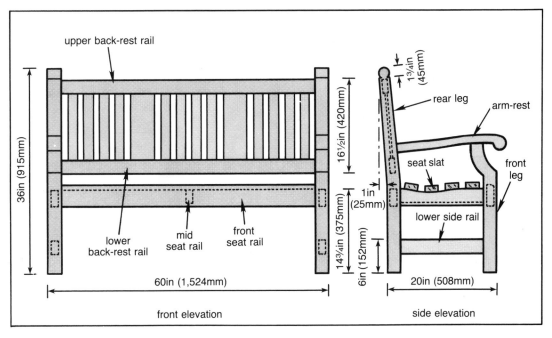

Front and side elevations.

So the choice comes down to one of the cheaper imported varieties of hardwood known for their strength, attractive grain and the ability to withstand all types of weather. Iroko or utile will give good results, and are hardwoods in the middle price range. The seat illustrated is made from utile which, like sapele, is a reasonably good substitute for mahogany, possessing a finely-structured grain with a pleasing reddish brown colour. Iroko, on the other hand, resembles teak.

The second point to consider is the size of the seat. You can decide for yourself whether your own garden seat should accommodate two, three or four persons. In terms of proportion, the best answer is the three-seater with an overall width of 60in (1,524mm), for this looks just right. However, you can alter the dimensions to make the seat wider or narrower, according to preference, remembering that the wider the seat becomes (and therefore the greater its seating capacity), so the larger must be the main components to bear the additional weight.

When viewed from the side, it is at once evident that the seat has a number of curved or angled parts, and it is important to know how these shapes are obtained before launching yourself into the work, so that the correct amount of wood can be calculated and purchased. The arm-rests and short side seat rails are not curved to any great extent, and may be cut from the specified cutting list sizes. The rear legs are raked back slightly, an angle being formed between the main part of the leg from the ground up to the seat, and the upper part that supports the back-rest. This, too, is quite a straightforward piece of shaping work.

The front legs are given the most pronounced curve at the point where they join the arm-rest. It is wise to economise in this case by marking the two front legs in alternate directions on a single piece of timber which must be cut considerably longer than the actual length of each individual leg to allow for the curves.

From the side elevation it can be seen that the rake of the rear legs, the curve at the top of the front legs and the shaping of the arm-rest all contribute to give each end-frame of the seat a complicated configuration, in which the accuracy of the joints is of paramount importance. You may prefer to draw a full-sized template on a large piece of card, so that these angles are reproduced exactly – but this is not strictly necessary.

You will, however, need templates for each of the front and rear legs, the arm-rest and the side seat rail, which is given a concave curve towards its rear end, with a dip of at least ½in (13mm), so that the seat slats undulate to give a comfortable sitting posture. Mark out all four templates on to thick card. Note that the rear leg is raked back at an angle so that the rear edge at the top lies 1in (25mm) further back than the lower vertical rear edge. The angle commences midway between the rear seat rail and the lower back-rest rail, or a distance of 16¼in (412mm) from the ground. There is also a slight tapering at the upper end of the leg when viewed from the side, and a decorative rounding effect at the top, with shallow shoulders cut in square.

The front leg, though shorter in length, is of a more complicated shape, with its inward-facing curve sweeping up to meet the lower edge of the arm-rest. Mark the curve on to the card with a pair of geometrical compasses, setting them to a radius of 7½in (190mm) for the outer curve, and 5in (127mm) for the inner.

The arm-rest, when viewed from the side, also has a rounded shape at the front end so that it comfortably receives the palm of the hand. There is a gentle concave dip along its upper surface with a corresponding curve worked along the lower surface to maintain a constant thickness of 2in (50mm) along most of its length before deepening at the front end to a diameter of 2⅜in (60mm) or so.

Remember that a tenon must be cut: at the top of each front leg, where the curve straightens out; at the rear end of the arm-rest; and at each end of the side seat rail. Allow an extra 1¾in (45mm) of material for this purpose when cutting these pieces roughly to length. You will later have to trim some of this back to suit the size of the individual tenons, but for the moment it ensures that you have sufficient length available. There is nothing worse than under-estimating the required length of a tenon, to find that it is too short.

Cut out the four templates with a sharp knife, laying them in place with respect to one another on a flat surface to check that they form an accurate pattern of the end-frame. Note that the lower side rail is missing, but as this is a straight length of timber with no shaping, there is no need to make a template for it.

Mark round each template in pencil on the corresponding lengths of material. You will recall that the two front legs are marked on a single piece of timber for the sake of economy, with the curves placed at opposite ends in alternating positions. The best tool for cutting all the shaped pieces to size is the jigsaw, fitted with a coarse blade to cut quickly through the wood. If you have access to a band saw, so much the better. Alternatively, you

can use a coping saw and achieve perfectly good results, but this will take you much longer. Whichever method you use, be sure to cut on the waste side of the pencil line, leaving a small amount to be trimmed by hand. Check that the blade of the saw is worked exactly at right-angles to the face of the wood, otherwise there will be the risk of serious under-cutting.

Manipulate the saw gradually around all the curved sections, taking extreme care to avoid scorching the wood. This is particularly a danger with high-speed

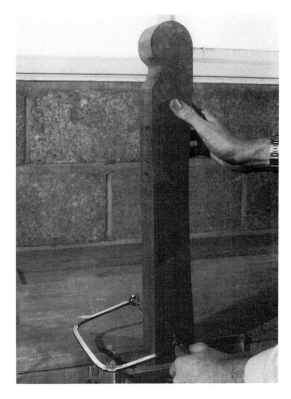

Remove the bulk of the waste from the main curved components with the coping saw or jigsaw. Here, the arm-rest is held firmly in the vice and cut to shape with the coping saw, working the blade carefully on the waste side of the pencil line.

power saws, due to the heat generated by friction. Remove the remaining waste with a spokeshave. Its chief usefulness is in being able to follow all the inside curves where an ordinary smoothing plane could never reach. As with any cutting instrument, the blade of the spokeshave must be kept very sharp and adjusted to the optimum setting for the best result. Finish off by rubbing down with medium-grade sandpaper.

The next step is to mark in and cut the mortise and tenon joints which, for the main part of the seat frame, are the pegged variety. With the development of reliable synthetic waterproof resin glues, which are well suited to outdoor furniture joints, there is not the same need for the pegs, but they remain to assist during assembly by the process known as draw-boring.

All the mortises used for jointing the main components of the frame need to be as large as possible, to give maximum strength. It is usual to arrange for the mortise to equal one-third the thickness of the pieces to be joined together, but in this case some of the pieces are of different thickness. For example, all the rails are narrower than the legs; only the arm-rest is the same. This does not matter greatly, and the most appropriate width for the mortises is ¾in (19mm). This is only slightly less than one-third the thickness of the arm-rest and the legs, which are 2½in (63mm) thick, and more than one-third the thickness of the rails, which are 1¾in (45mm) and 1¼in (32mm) thick depending on the rail.

Set the spurs of the mortise gauge to a gap of ¾in (19mm), and adjust the fence so that they mark at the centre of the legs. Now measure in the positions of the two side rails on both the front and rear

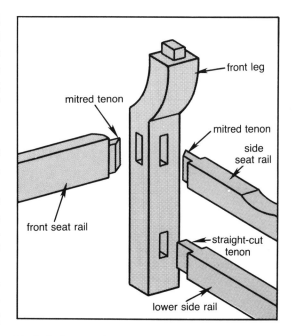

Exploded view of mortise and tenon joints for rails to front leg. The same arrangement is used to joint them to the rear leg.

legs, and mark them with a pencil and square. The length of the mortise is determined by the width of the rails, which gives the width of the tenon, and these are different; the side seat rails being 2¾in (70mm) wide, and the lower side rail 2½in (63mm) wide.

Having set the limits of the mortises according to the width of the rails, scribe two parallel lines between the squared pencil markings with the spurs of the mortise gauge. Similarly, mark in the mortise positions for the long front and back seat rails and the back-rest rails. The seat rail mortises are each set at exactly the same height as the mortises for the side seat rail in both front and rear legs, and these are cut in such a way that the mortises meet within the wood.

The back-rest mortises are slightly different, because the raked part of the rear leg has a tapered profile, so that the upper end is narrower than the lower part where the raked angle begins. This does not create any real problem, as it is simply a question of re-setting the fence of the mortise gauge so that its two spurs mark centrally at the top of the leg, just below the rounded end-grain. Use this same setting to scribe the mortise lines for both top and bottom back-rest rails, working the gauge from the forward edge of the leg.

As the joints need to be as strong as possible, it is our intention to make the mortises equal in length to the width of the rails – in other words, the tenons should only have two shoulders instead of four. This does, however, lead to one small problem. If you cut the mortises exactly on the marked pencil lines, they usually work out slightly larger than you intend due to the wood's habit of compressing as the chisel cuts into it. This can actually mean that you end up with mortises which are longer than the width of the tenons, and small gaps will be visible at each end. To avoid this, set in each mortise by $\frac{1}{16}$in (2mm). You need not bother to pencil this in, but make a point of working the chisel by this amount inside the marked area.

The quickest way of removing the waste from the mortise is to drill a series of holes along its length using a centre bit fractionally smaller in diameter than the width of the finished joint. A $\frac{5}{8}$in (16mm)-diameter drill bit is best for this purpose. Mount it firmly in the hand-brace, and place a depth-guide on the stem of the bit a distance of $1\frac{5}{8}$in (41mm) from the cutting tip. The depth-guide need be no more than a piece of sticky tape bound round the stem, so that you know when to stop drilling.

Bore a series of holes along the marked-out area of the mortise, pausing often to clear out the accumulating scraps of wood. Chop out the remaining waste with a $\frac{3}{4}$in (19mm) chisel and mallet, cutting to the required depth of $1\frac{5}{8}$in (41mm), and working the chisel carefully to ensure that the sides and ends of the mortise are vertical. Where two adjoining mortises meet inside the wood, their sides should coincide at right-angles and the ends merge without any ridges between them.

Now for the rail tenons. Remember that there are two rail thicknesses – $1\frac{3}{4}$in (45mm) and $1\frac{1}{4}$in (32mm). Taking the seat and back-rest rails first, begin by cutting all the long rails to length, squaring off at the shoulder positions with pencil lines. Having originally allowed at least $1\frac{3}{4}$in (45mm) for the tenons, trim these back to $1\frac{5}{8}$in (41mm), giving an overall length of $58\frac{1}{4}$in (1,480mm) for the long rails and $18\frac{1}{4}$in (464mm) for the side rails.

Adjust the mortise gauge fence to scribe its parallel lines centrally across the $1\frac{3}{4}$in (45mm)-thick edge of the four long rails. The two back-rest rails are both $2\frac{3}{4}$in (70mm) wide, and so is the rear seat rail, but the front seat rail is wider, at $3\frac{3}{4}$in (95mm). Mark in the tenons, then clamp each piece in the work-bench vice and remove the waste with the tenon saw to form the two shoulders.

Make a trial fitting of each joint. Having cut the mortises marginally shorter than the width of the rails, and hence the height of the tenons, you may now need to trim the tenons at the top and bottom, effectively cutting a pair of shallow secondary shoulders, until the two parts of the joint slide easily together. The front seat rail being much wider than the length of its mortise, you must cut a deep third shoulder at the top before the joint will fit.

At this stage, it is not possible to assemble the long seat rails and side seat rails fully into their adjacent mortises at the same time, because each tenon blocks the full entry of its partner. The solution is to cut mitres at the end of each pair. Loosely assemble both end-frames, consisting of the front and rear leg, the side seat rail and the lower side rail, and place the arm-rest in position according to its correct height. Because the rear end of the arm-rest joins the rear leg at a point where the leg is raked backwards, it is

advisable to mount it at a slight angle so that it meets the rear leg perpendicularly.

Mark in the mortise on the back leg, and the tenon at the rear end of the arm-rest, cutting these to the same 1⅝in (41mm) depth, and make a trial fitting. Re-assemble the end-frame components again and, with the arm-rest aligned accurately against the rear leg, mark a pencil line across the front leg to indicate the depth of the tenon and pencil in the limits of the mortise. There will be a small amount of movement in this joint, as it is the last one to be cut, so you are advised to set the length of the mortise to 2in (50mm) and no more, keeping it well inside the width of the front leg.

Assembling the end-frame.

The mortise cannot be cut as deeply in the arm-rest as in the other members, and a depth of 1¼in (32mm) is recommended. Cut out both parts of the joint, and fit the arm-rest in place to complete the end-frame assembly.

Before sawing the mid-seat rail and back-rest slats to length, it is advisable to check the temporarily assembled seat so that its frame can be seen to be standing square on flat ground with all joints fitting fully and accurately. Measure the distances between the front and back seat rails, and the top and bottom back-rest rails. Note that the main part of the mid-seat rail will need to be longer than both the side seat rails, once you discount the tenon at each end, because the front and back seat rails are set back by ⅜in (9mm) from the inside edges of the front and rear legs. The total rail length is the same, but the mortises in the rails are not cut as deeply as those in the legs, so the tenons are not as long.

There is a further difference between the single mid-seat rail and its two side seat rail partners. It is cut from a smaller cross-section of material, equal in size to that used for the lower side rails. However, you can use the same cardboard template to mark in the dip, and the same method as for the previous curved surfaces, sawing away the bulk of the waste, shaping with the spokeshave and smoothing with sandpaper.

Dismantle the frame of the seat to separate the two long seat rails and the two back-rest rails. The front and back seat rails are of differing widths, the front one being wider than the back so that its uppermost edge is aligned with that of the four seat slats. Measure the mid-point along the length of both rails to give the position of the mid-seat rail.

Before marking in the mortises at these mid-point positions, consider the following important differences which distinguish this particular pair of joints from all those used in the construction of the main frame. In all the previous joints, the mortise was cut to the same length as the width of the tenon rail so that the tenon had only two shoulders. But this arrangement, whilst being ideally suited to the joints between the rails, arm-rests and legs where there is sufficient surrounding wood to absorb all downward loading, is unsuitable for the joints between the mid-seat rail and the two long seat rails because it would mean placing the mortise much too near to the bottom edge of the long rails, leading to potential weakness under load – that is, when the seat is in use.

In this instance, the mortises are cut shorter than the total width of the mid-seat rail, being set in by ⅜in (9mm) top and bottom. Note that the mid-seat rail is not as wide as the two rails to which it is jointed, so that it is set up from both bottom edges in order for the curved top edge to be level with the back seat rail. When you add this ¼in (6mm) difference to the setting in of the second pair of tenon shoulders by ⅜in (9mm), you will find that the lower end of each mortise is ⅝in (16mm) from the bottom edge of the rails in which it is cut, which is ample.

The width of the mortise and the thickness of its corresponding tenon is ¾in (19mm), as with all the other main joints. Mark in the two mortises using a pencil and square, scribing the tenon lines with the mortise gauge. Before cutting the joints, check all your markings to make sure that the mid-seat rail is set at exactly the same height as the two side seat rails.

Cut the two mortises initially with the

handbrace fitted with the ⅝in (16mm)-diameter centre bit, chopping out the remainder of the waste with the ¾in (19mm) chisel and mallet to a depth of 1¼in (32mm). Saw the two pairs of shoulders for each tenon with the tenon saw. It may be necessary to pare the tenons down slightly with the chisel until they fit fully into their mortises. Knock both joints together so that the three rails form an H-shape.

Re-assemble the two long seat rails to the end-frames of the seat, and check that the mid-seat rail lies at the same height as the two side seat rails, with the curves in perfect alignment. This is best ascertained by laying one of the seat slats across all three rails. If the mid-seat rail is found to be too high, you can trim the bottom cheek of the tenons to drop it slightly, packing the space above with thin strips cut from waste material. Conversely, if the rail is too low, trim the uppermost cheek and pack below.

Next, fit the slats between the top and bottom back-rest rails. The total number used in my example is twelve narrow slats and two wide slats, arranged at regular intervals into the pattern four-one-four-one-four. If you wish, you could alter this to a pattern of your own choice, but you should bear in mind that it would be a mistake to economise on the number of slats by arranging them at wider intervals, because this will only result in the back-rest appearing far too open.

To determine the exact distance between each of the slats, measure the width of one wide slat and multiply this by two, then measure the width of a narrow slat and multiply by twelve. Add these two amounts together to give the total width of all the slats, subtracting

this from the length of the back-rest rails minus their tenons, giving the overall space that will be left open. That should test your mathematical skills! This figure, in inches or millimetres, must now be divided by fifteen (the number of gaps between the rear legs), leaving you with the width of each individual opening. You will find it much easier to work in metric.

If the resulting measurement is not an exact round figure in millimetres, but works out as a fraction instead, you ought to be able to judge this on your tape-measure to ensure that the gaps are all the same. But to safeguard against the possibility of compounding a small error with each measurement in moving from one end of the rail to the other, start from the centre and work outwards in both directions so that any slight inaccuracy will only show in the two gaps occurring at the two furthermost ends, maintaining the basic symmetry.

Mark in a series of lines with the square and pencil along the lower edge of the top back-rest rail, and the upper edge of the bottom back-rest rail, to define the limits of all the slots, carefully checking the four–one–four–one–four configuration as you go along. Each slat is fitted in place between the two back-rest rails with mortise and tenon joints, the mortise being equal in length to the width of the relevant slat, and ½in (13mm) wide. Set the spurs of the mortise gauge to a corresponding gap of ½in (13mm), and adjust the fence so that the mortises are set ⅜in (9mm) back from the forward face of the two rails. Mark in each of the fourteen mortises for both rails, taking care not to scribe the lines over the gaps between the slats, confining them to the slat positions only.

As with previous mortises, it is the intention to cut them to equal the width of the slats, but as a precaution you should cut the extreme ends of each mortise fractionally within the marked zone, because the chisel usually compresses the wood as it is driven into the cross-grain, as described earlier, resulting in the mortise being slightly longer than you intend.

Cut all the mortises to a depth of ½in (13mm), using the same technique all the way along both rails: start by drilling a series of holes with a ⅜in (9mm)-diameter centre bit, then chop out the waste with the ½in (13mm) chisel. Measure and cut all the slats to length, marking in the tenon at each end with the mortise gauge, re-setting its fence so that the spurs scribe centrally across the ¾in (19mm) thickness of the slats. This will give shoulders ⅛in (3mm) deep. Because these are so shallow, you will have to use a different method to prepare them.

Clamp each slat down flat near the end of the work-bench, or hold it firmly in the bench hook, and saw along the shoulder line to a depth of ⅛in (3mm) with the tenon saw. Then take the ½in (13mm) chisel and gently tap it along the scribed line on the end-grain until the wood begins to split. Work the chisel carefully along the entire width of the slat, prising the waste away. Clean off any remaining waste with a paring action of the chisel to leave well-defined shoulders.

Fit each slat into its appropriate mortise, trimming where necessary to achieve a perfect fit, and make a trial assembly of the two back-rest rails once all fourteen slats are in place. Now fit the entire assembly to both end-frames to check that the four main joints still line up accurately, allowing for the fact that the presence of the slats may now make a slight difference to the distance between the two back-rest rails, either setting them closer or further apart than when they were originally assembled without the slats. If the joints fail to fit accurately, trim the tenons at each end of the two back-rest rails until the whole back-rest assembly slots fully and easily into position between the two end-frames.

The next stage is to prepare the seat slats. These are first measured to the required length, and cut with the jigsaw to give a smooth end-grain. Lay them in place across the temporarily assembled seat frame to check that they are equal to the full width of the seat. Mark the screw hole positions at both ends of each slat so that they are located exactly half-way across the width of the slat, and also half-way across the thickness of the two seat rails. There is no need to screw the seat slats to the mid-seat rail, because you will only succeed in placing a row of screws in a rather prominent part of the seat, where somebody will eventually sit upon them to their discomfort!

Drill the holes at the end of the slats with a number 10 woodscrew bit. Do not attempt to countersink the top of each hole, because the screws used for assembly will be fitted with matching cup washers for neatness and added strength. Screw a mild steel 2½in (63mm) number 10 woodscrew into each hole to cut the thread, until the tip of the screw just emerges on the under-side of the slats. Arrange all four slats on the seat, measuring them carefully to set them at equal distances from one another, and by the same distance from the front and back seat rails. This may need some calculation, as with the setting apart of the back-rest slats, and in this case the dis-

The slats for the back-rest are fitted between the two back-rest rails with two-shouldered mortise and tenon joints.

The four seat slats are fastened to the side seat rails with brass screws and cup washers.

tances are a little more difficult to measure due to the dip along the top edge of the three short seat rails.

When you have placed the slats in the required positions, give each screw one or two turns with a short screwdriver – a vital tool, as there is only limited space beneath the arm-rest – so that a small impression is left on both the rails. Identify each slat by making a pencil reference mark to distinguish them from one another, and dismantle the seat entirely.

Clamp the side seat rails in the vice and drill out the marked hole positions with the same number 10 drill bit to a depth of 1¼in (32mm). Take the front seat rail and chamfer the top edge to form a slope towards the front face. As a guide to how much you should chamfer, set the marking gauge to ⅜in (9mm) and scribe this along the upper front face. Plane down to this line, with the chamfer extending approximately two-thirds of the way back across the thickness of the rail.

Rub down all the seat components with medium-grade sandpaper, paying particular attention to the curved surfaces so that all marks left by the spokeshave are completely erased to leave a perfectly smooth finish. Sandpaper all the edges (except for those where two joints meet), to round them off.

The seat is assembled in stages, beginning with the two end-frames, followed by the back-rest assembly, then joining together the end-frames with the four long rails, and finally mounting the seat slats. Before assembly can commence, however, there is one last step needed to complete the preparation of the main mortise and tenon joints. This is the process known as draw-boring.

To put it simply, all the joints that are

formed between the four legs, two arm-rests and eight main rails are secured in place with small wooden pegs cut from hardwood dowelling. Most of the joints have two pegs each, but some of the smaller joints, such as those cut in the arm-rests and the lower side rails, have only one peg apiece. The term 'draw-boring' means that when the holes are drilled for the pegs in both the mortise and the tenon, instead of the drillings passing through in a continuous straight line, the hole in the tenon is deliberately set slightly out of line so that the peg, when it is driven into the joint, pulls the two parts tightly together.

Start by measuring and drilling all the holes that pass through the mortises. These are all marked on the outward-facing part of the legs and the arm-rests, and are set in by ⅜in (9mm) from the edge adjacent to the mortise. Where only one peg is to be used, this is placed centrally through the side of the mortise; for two pegs, these are set in by ½in (13mm) from the ends of the mortise.

Clamp the piece firmly to the work-bench and drill vertically down through

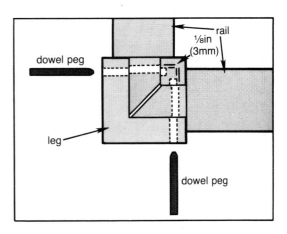

Method of draw-boring.

the mortise with a ¼in (6mm)-diameter centre bit in such a way that the drill bit breaks through on one side of the mortise and crosses its width before boring further into the other side. The hole should be drilled to a total depth of 1¾in (45mm).

Having completed the mortise holes, fit the appropriate tenon fully into position and pass a nail or some other suitable marking device – the bradawl will probably be too short to reach – down the hole to mark its centre on one cheek of the tenon. Dismantle the joint again and adjust the centre of the tenon hole from the mark made by the nail so that it is ¹⁄₁₆in (2mm) nearer to the shoulder. Cut the wooden pegs from ¼in (6mm)-diameter dowelling, preparing each peg to a length of 2in (50mm). Chamfer one end by giving a few twists in a pencil sharpener – without this, the peg will be unable to carry out its function.

Mix a quantity of waterproof resin wood glue, and apply it by brush to the mortises and tenons of all the component parts for one end-frame, tapping the joints together with the mallet and a block of clean scrap wood. Glue the pegs, and drive them into their holes, one by one, leaving ¼in (6mm) or so projecting clear of the surface. Wipe away any excess glue from around the joints with a damp rag, and place the assembly to one side for at least twenty-four hours for the glue to harden. After this period has elapsed, trim off the ends of the dowel pegs with a sharp chisel so that they are flush with the surrounding wood, and finish off with sandpaper. Assemble the second end-frame likewise, checking that it makes a perfect match with the first end-frame.

When both end-frames are complete, proceed to assembling the back-rest, gluing all the slats into place between the two rails. Knock the joints fully home, and check that they are all square. Glue the joints at one end of the two back-rest rails, and assemble this end to its corresponding end-frame, draw-boring the joints with their glued dowel pegs.

Next, glue the mid-seat rail into position between the front and back seat rails, then apply glue to the joints at the same end of the two long rails as that for the back-rest rails, assembling to the same end-frame. Finally, glue the joints for the second end-frame, knock these into place, and add the pegs. When the glue has completely set, and all the pegs been trimmed back flush with the frame, rub down the entire seat with medium and fine-grade sandpaper to remove all traces of it from around the joints.

Before adding the four seat slats, give the seat frame two or three applications of wood finish, rubbing well into the wood with a clean soft cloth. There are various shades available, and you should choose one that matches closely the natural colour of the wood. Apply the same finish to all surfaces of the seat slats, including the end-grain.

After the treatment has dried, assemble the seat slats to the seat frame. It is best to remove the steel screws which were originally used to cut the thread, and replace them with 2½in (63mm) number 10 brass screws and matching brass cup washers. Brass screws were not fitted at the outset because brass is a relatively soft alloy, and the slot of the screw will easily get damaged if the screwdriver meets any resistance in the first fitting of the screw.

So now the garden seat is finished, and

it only remains to add one or two words of advice. Even with a durable hardwood and a good water-resisting finish, it pays not to let the seat stand permanently on grass. For one thing, it will not do the grass much good. If you wish the seat to take its position on the lawn, place small pieces of paving stone beneath the legs. You could add small steel or brass 'domes of silence' to the bottom end-grain of each leg, thereby ensuring that the woodwork always remains clear of the ground.

Exposure to sun, wind and rain inevitably has the effect of weathering wood, no matter how well it is protected. Make a point of giving the seat an annual treatment with a wood finish, or some such similar substance, to keep it looking at its best.

Index